D1085821

Forew

Strap in my friends because you are about to take a ride that will thrill you, challenge you and embolden you to take action. *She Who Rises* is a journey framed with four important destinations; Essence, Explore, Eliminate, and Expand. Together they capture the honest and transparent experiences of a Leader, Coach, Pastor, Mother and Wife. What sets this book apart is the depth of authenticity and personal soul searching that are contained in these pages.

In the author's own words this book, "unleashes you to become the woman you are created to be — powerful, visionary, and joyful." Though written through the eyes of this insightful woman, the principles and strategies contained in this book are universal. The questions at the end of each chapter make this resource a living document that you will return to time and time again for strength and wisdom.

This resource leads us through an incredible journey of fatigue, faith and favor that accompanies the fast pace of a driven pursuit of life and lands us in newly discovered renewal and refocusing. Lia claims the steps of her journey in ways that are instructive and life-giving. Her perspectives for working through things are so real that they pounce on the reader with a, "Why didn't I think of that?"

It has been my privilege to journey with Lia as her coach, colleague and friend. These three lenses of her passionate pursuit of life are reflected in this resource in a way that empowers you, equips you and guides you in the way that only a true friend can do.

This book ends with a beginning, a renewed promise to discover God's best for you and those who are entrusted to your care. - *Rev. Dr. Rodney Thomas Smothers, Leadership Coach*

On a Wednesday night, during prayer, Lia Mcintosh and I entered into a divine space of healing. Although, she was a student pastor her prayer life displayed a direct connection to God. She was determined to intercede on the behalf of the broken, lost, and confused. Lia and I developed a friendship that was orchestrated by God. I have had the privilege to be apart of watching Lia's growth over the years as she served as my pastor and mentor. This book describes the woman who rises from within despite her circumstances. Use Lia's coaching techniques and her truth to unleash the warrior chick inside of you. The time is now. Let's rise!

Rochinda Pickens, Author, From Being Kept to Being Kept, www.keptwomanofgod.com

With *She Who Rises,* Lia McIntosh gifts us with a passionate, powerful, and personal testimony to the abundant life that we can all live - if we will only redefine the rules. McIntosh provides a realigning wake up call and a roadmap that leads from exhaustion to empowerment. Grab your BFFs and embark upon the *She Who Rises* journey together as you discover the "Warrior Chick" within! - *Rev. Jasmine R. Smothers, Co-Author, Not Safe For Church: Ten Commandments for Reaching New Generations .www.jasminesmothers.org*

iv

The title alone, *She Who Rises* would pique the interest of most women who are silently crying out of despair, not living the life God has for them. The author's transparency into her own struggles of insecurities, fears, and pains of becoming a mother and living authentically, while the world viewed her as successful, invites the readers to get real with their own struggles. This inspiring book was skillfully written in how it's primary focus is to help women walk in their calling, but also part devotional and part autobiography. It's eloquently expressed, complete with tools and exercises, biblical perspective, and resources to help in living your authentic life. No longer ignore that voice inside of you begging the question, "Is there more?" Your Warrior Chick is calling! – *Carlotta Berry, Poet*

With this book Lia seeks to motivate the reader to find their true passion in life. She uses her life experiences to illustrate how to overcome difficult times and move forward. This book is the result of an ordinary woman who is a nice person and who "gets it." Read this true life story, follow the coaching suggestions, and all will be better persons. Enjoy.

- Louis Virdure, Coach, Professor, Attorney (retired) and Lia's dad

Dedication

This book is dedicated with love to my parents, Mildred and Louis Virdure, and all those who have contributed to my joy of life through coaching, mentoring, and encouraging me along the way. To my brother Anthony, whose presence in my life has always been a gift.

With special gratitude to my husband Kevin and mother-in-law Wanda, whose unwavering love, encouragement and prayers enable me to rise up daily and become the woman God calls me to be.

And to our children, Isaac, Aaron and Alexis, each whom have a special place in my heart and continually inspire me. I am because you are.

Table of Contents

Part III: Eliminate

How to discern and cut out limiting beliefs and actions that block a RISEN life?

Part IV: Expand

How to practice and share the RISEN life?

Epilogue
About the Author

SHE WHO RISES

Introduction

I am grateful you are here. It is no accident. God is at work in your life, and there is something here God wants you to understand and act upon as a result of the journey through this book. As women, sisters, wives, mothers, entrepreneurs, and leaders, we pour out our hearts and souls for many. We are committed to making the lives of others better at home, work, church, and in the world. Yet, we are sometimes quietly suffering. Outwardly, we are smiling and sometimes successful but inwardly, we are often perpetually exhausted and wondering if there is more to life. As Richard Rohr in his book Falling Upward writes, "We know there is a further journey, an invitation from our soul, or even a deep obedience to God." This book is for women like you and me who are ready to live a more fulfilling and empowered life. Greg McKeown in his book Essentialism: The Disciplined Pursuit of Less asked a question that captures the essence of this invitation, "What if we stopped celebrating being busy as a measurement of importance? What if instead we celebrated how much time we had spent listening, pondering, meditating, and enjoying time with the most important people in our lives?" What if we measured success by how faithfully we've pursued God's purpose and not external accomplishments?

So what will it take to get there?

The purpose of this book is to unleash you to become the woman you are created to be --- powerful, visionary, and joyful. This is a path toward significance internally and success externally. It will be an incredible journey. Though it will take effort, it will bring you joy and peace like never before because you'll know and live your life's purpose. This is the path to unleash the Warrior Chick inside of you!

As we begin this journey consider making three important shifts in your life.

1. *Set aside 30 minutes a day for "Me Time."* During this time set aside your phone, email, and other distractions. Create a quiet place and space to rest, pray, and journey through this book. It is purposefully designed to be a workbook to support you in claiming your dreams, discerning your gifts, and living them out powerfully. Many people desire outward greatness in the form of successful businesses, organizational recognition, and financial freedom without doing the internal work. A lack of alignment between one's inner character and outward persona inevitably manifests crises, inwardly or outwardly. This journey purposefully begins inward and then moves outward so that your success will be sustainable when opposition, uncertainty, and challenges emerge. Give yourself the gift of thirty minutes a day of "Me Time." Stop now, put it on your schedule, grab a cup of tea and let's journey together.

What time each day will you set aside as "me time"?

_____

_____

_____

_____

_____

2. ***Invite a Friend to Journey with You.*** During the writing of this book, I was reminded of the value of friendship. All of the lessons I've learned thus far on my journey have been with someone who helped me clarify thinking, dream bigger and see broader than I could alone. Friends provide a compassionate, secure and trusted outlet to vent problems and provide support through conflict. My friends have been sisters and coaches, mentors and therapists, some paid and some unpaid. Most of all, they have been available to journey with me and remind me to keep going. You will face the temptation to give up, trivialize yourself, and play small. Yet, together we will emerge, soar, and accept our wisdom, strength, and beauty.

Who will journey with you?

_____

_____

_____

_____

3. ***Reward yourself once per week with an activity that feeds your soul.*** This journey towards significance and success will sometimes be challenging, so intentionally infuse your journey with joy.

How will you reward yourself each week? What types of activities feed your soul?

_____

_____

_____

_____

_____

After a decade working as a pastor, Bible teacher, business and nonprofit leader, I found that many people secretly battle feelings of being trapped, powerless, alone, and insignificant. We experience chaos, rejection, depression and boredom. Yet, something in our soul tells us we are created for much more. Too often people are stuck in a rut of daily activities, all of which may be good and necessary, but are just the beginning of life, not the fullness of who we really are. This motivated me to write She Who Rises: Unleashing the Warrior Chick Within.

On the morning of April 6, 2006, I was lying on the doctor's exam table for a dilation and curettage (D&C). A surgical procedure often performed after a first-trimester miscarriage. I had been diagnosed days before as having a miscarriage. This was my third miscarriage in two years and I was heartbroken. My husband Kevin and I had been on a four-year journey trying to conceive a child. We hoped and believed this pregnancy would be different, yet my hope was slowly vanishing. In the wake of our struggles with infertility, I found myself going from doctor to doctor, hormone treatment to egg follicle stimulation. The result was extreme emotional and physical exhaustion. A nurse at the infertility clinic said to me, "You've got to slow down." I thought to myself, what does she know about my life? But that wise statement, spoken more than ten years ago, still resonates with me today. She was right. My diagnosis was "unexplained infertility." Based on all the physical tests, I should have been able to conceive, but realistically my body's ability to ovulate fruitfully had shut down. The doctors told me to gain a bit of weight, slow down, and come back in a few months for more tests. After three miscarriages, I was devastated and realized I no longer had the answer to fix this situation on my own.

I was forced to ask myself, what was the purpose of my toil? Why was I running myself ragged? Was this the fullness of joy my faith promised? Was this the life I wanted? I was traveling constantly, answering emails until late in the evening, pouring myself into church work and launching a successful beauty and wellness business in my spare time. But my life, I realized, was being sucked away. On an airplane to Cincinnati, Ohio, early one Monday morning, a trip I'd made dozens of times before, I wrote my "transition plan."

By traditional measures, of money and influence, I was successful. But, I had a deep sense there was more to life. I could not keep this pace. I knew something had to drastically change. My husband, Kevin knew it also, because our marriage was suffering.

At the age of sixteen, I started working in corporate America for an international consumer products company, in St. Louis, as a sales intern. It was the summer before my senior year in high school. What followed was four summer internships during college, and twelve years of climbing the corporate ladder towards a lucrative career. I was promoted on average every two years and my salary, which started at $34,000, grew above six figures after twelve years. I was awarded stock options, travel bonuses, and invitations to elite leadership training experiences. On the outside, everything looked great. Inside, my soul was depleted.

This was my wake-up call. Up until that point, I followed the rules. I worked hard and found intermittent fulfillment in promotions, awards, and travel. Yet, I was restless, searching for a new journey. In a strange way, I knew I could not stay where I was. I did not know exactly what that meant, but I felt an urgency to leave the perceived comforts of my corporate job. I even contemplated leaving my marriage to be free. I did leave that corporate job. Not because there was anything wrong with the job (although I was burnt out on all the travel). I was being called to a new journey that I could not ignore. I recommitted to our marriage, because I realized my husband was not my problem. In fact, he was to be my companion on the journey.

That day, April 6, 2006, everything changed. Instead of a miscarriage, the doctor discovered a baby's heartbeat! Our first child was seven weeks old in my womb. What began as a tragic day ended up, by the grace of God, being a day of joy. There is no other way to explain it. After four years of infertility treatments, our first child was conceived naturally, just when we were about to give up hope. Seven months later, a healthy baby boy, Isaac Jordan, was born. Two years later, Aaron Micah was born adding a double blessing to our family. And in 2012, Alexis Marie, our baby girl was born. Needless to say, our lives have never been the same.

In six years, we had three children. During that time, I completed a Masters of Divinity degree, was ordained a United Methodist Elder, and founded a new church. Kevin completed his MBA, coached little league football, and provided me support every step of the way.

I still had one huge problem...ex-haust-ion. I was working, mothering, and living at a non-stop pace and I was physically, emotionally, and spiritually exhausted. The word exhaustion according to the New Oxford American Dictionary means, "to draw off or out, to use up completely, make weak or helpless, as by fatigue." I bet you know what I'm talking about. Exhaustion, the physical dis-ease I felt and you feel, is not a delusion. Our bodies speak out of fatigue. The mental weariness is real. Creativity is fleeting because our minds are cluttered. Emotional numbness sets in. Spiritually, the well of inspiration is desert dry and panting for water.

Extreme cases of exhaustion are often referred to as burnout, resulting from excessive and prolonged stress on the body, mind, and soul. It's what I feel after a fifteen-hour day of working and caring for family. I literally can't go anymore. It's like walking dead. Even if you wouldn't claim that you're "burned out", perhaps you're dangerously close and ready for a different way of life. The good news is these feelings of dis-ease are signs to get our attention. They are our souls speaking, saying, stop, look and listen. Your soul is desperate for something more.

I know what it's like to be excited by great vision, but feel too tired to fully live into it. That's why I've written this resource for busy people just like you and me who are ready for a different purpose and pace. Yes, this book is to set you free. It will equip you to live a life of fulfillment in soul and self and unleash your gifts to bless others powerfully. That's what rising and being empowered is all about. To be authentically you, fulfilling your dreams with ease and grace, not exhaustion, is your destiny.

For me, the woman who rises, is a warrior chick. It's that chick who is confident and vulnerable, courageous and wise, decisive yet collaborative, and inspired to transform the world. It's that chick who's not intimidated by nor needs to be affirmed by others to live her dreams. She is fierce yet humble. She is a warrior. This book is about unleashing this woman, the warrior within you.

I first began to discover my warrior chick when I ran cross-country in high school. Competing at the varsity level required running six days a week, sometimes twice a day, with my dad and brother. During the height of the season, we'd run the "East St. Louis Hills" early on Sunday mornings. This was the name for our longer eight-mile run of the week. This run was called the "East St. Louis Hills" because the East St. Louis runners were some of the baddest competitors in our AAU summer track program. Running hills at home was preparation to run with the most talented competitors. I was learning to be a warrior chick, fiercely committed to unleashing the dream within and maximizing her gifts from God.

In Biblical scripture, I think of warrior chicks like Mary who birthed Jesus despite the social costs. Mary Magdalene who loved Jesus and served him passionately despite her past. Deborah, a judge, prophet, and dedicated leader, who despite the rarity of women in leadership in biblical history, led the Israelites to victory.

Stop for a moment and write about the fierce woman who resides deep inside your soul. What's her name? What is she like?

_____

_____

_____

_____

_____

_____

_____

_____

_____

Now, let's continue the journey through this book using your inner warrior to fuel your progress. It, like all journeys, will be challenging and require sacrifice. However, if you go all in, you'll discover revelations about yourself that can be life transforming.

This journey is designed to be taken in 40 days. Each day of this journey will contain three important elements:

First, a unique aspect of power and love will be discussed. Read each of these carefully and be open to a new understanding of what it means to be powerful, visionary, and joyful.

Second, you will be given a specific question or action to complete. Some will be easy and some very challenging. But take each invitation seriously.

Third, you will be given journal space to capture what you're learning and doing. It is important that you take advantage of this space to capture what is happening to you along the way. These notes will document your progress and affirm that you are journeying forward. Remember, you have the power to chart your journey. Don't give up. Learning to emerge fully as the person you are is one of the most important things you'll ever do.

We'll journey through this book in four parts.

Part I: Essence: What is the core mindset of one who RISES?

Part II: Explore: How to cultivate a life that RISES?

Part III: Eliminate: How to discern and cut out limiting beliefs and actions that block a RISEN life?

Part IV: Expand: How to practice and share the RISEN life?

Essential to this journey is acknowledging the stirring inside of you and developing an intimate relationship with God. Through that relationship, your purpose will become clearer. Boldness and courage will emerge as God reveals your true self. That is the place of freedom. I'm honored to journey with you. Let's go.

Part I: Essence

What is the core mindset of one who RISES?

In the U.S., we live in a culture that thrives on fast. Just look at the marketing of fast food restaurants to see its impact. McDonald's marketing slogan is "good food fast." It does not promise great food, but fast food. As a mother of three young children, with busy school and sport schedules, we roll through the drive-thru of McDonald's on early Saturday mornings, late weekday nights and anytime we need a quick happy meal. Often we order a cheeseburger, chicken nuggets, a southwest chicken salad and, of course, a McFlurry to top it off. McDonald's and other fast food restaurants are a convenience and a necessity to help meet the demands of our hurried lives. At least McDonald's has a few healthier options like apples, oatmeal, yogurt and salads to make us feel a little better about our obsession with food, fast.

Unfortunately, the downside of our fast food lifestyle is we forget how to slow down. We forget the pleasures of cooking dinner and sitting down to eat together at the table. We forget the joy of smelling the aroma of chicken and vegetables cooking for hours in the Crock-Pot. Likewise, we ignore the cry of our souls for rest, quiet reflection and worship. Yet, I've found that it is in the quiet solitude of life that we are able to slow down, rest in God, and make room for our souls to expand. In that space, God shapes our thoughts and recreates us. In quiet spaces, we detach from life's expectations for fast results, and the need for approval by others and reattach to God's acceptance, love, and peace. This is the core of what She Who Rises is about.

The mindset of one who rises is not about finding a faster way to do one more thing. It is a different, empowering way of being and doing life. Yet, internalizing this way of being is not necessarily easy when we have been trained to work hard and achieve more to prove our worth. The following ten truths in Part 1 of this book are foundational to the ability to rise and soar.

1. Live in Expectation
2. Be Empowered
3. Make Progress not Perfection
4. Focus on Quality not Quantity
5. Be Courageous
6. Claim Your Vision
7. Be Proactive not Reactive
8. Keep Hope Alive
9. Know Your Story
10. Redefine Success

Each concept challenges a myth and replaces it with a truth. Embracing, living and sharing these truths will free you to pursue what really matters. They will enable you to live at your highest level of purpose, vision and joy. Finally, at the end of each truth are coaching exercises and questions to support you in living a risen life. Ready. Set. Go.

1.   Live in Expectation

As a little girl, I remember looking up at the clouds in the blue sky asking the question, "What do you see?" I saw images like elephants, space ships and bananas. Oh, what fun! It's amazing what people are able to discern or "see" when we allow ourselves to comprehend beyond our first glance because we're expecting more. Scripture says in Psalm 34:8a, "Taste and see that the Lord is good..." That's what expectation is all about. It's a desire to taste and see what God is up to in your life. It's the ability to listen to your heart and take courageous steps forward. It's the ability to separate what others want you to do from what you really would love to be doing with your life. Importantly, expecting is a verb. It's a practice we are called to cultivate daily.

As I'm writing this, we are mere weeks away from Christmas and there is an excitement in the air. We are expecting great things. We give and receive gifts at Christmas, celebrate the birth of Jesus and find many reasons to celebrate. What are you expecting for Christmas this year? Your birthday? Anniversary? We can use that same expectation in our lives everyday as well.

Myth: Reality never lives up to my expectations.

Truth: I expect and believe great things are coming.

Coaching Practice:

If you could have anything, be anything, or do anything, what would it be? Write down everything that comes to mind and be as specific as possible. Do not feel the need to be realistic or justify your dreams. Just write.

_____

_____

_____

_____

_____

_____

_____

_____

_____

_____

How will you celebrate when you've made progress on your dreams?

_____

_____

_____

_____

_____

_____

_____

_____

_____

_____

That's the power of expectation.

2.   Be Empowered

As a freshman in college, my first job was in the bakery of my dormitory. I would wake at 5 am to help prepare breakfast for hundreds of students. It was so early that the dorm elevators were still turned off, so I had to take the stairs to the bottom floor of the building for work. I took the job because my dad said he worked in food service during his college years. He also assured me that working early mornings before my classes would free up my entire day for other activities. I hated that job in the bakery. I lasted maybe three months before I quit after burning my forearm on a hot pan of biscuits. I also despised waking up at 5 am before all the other students to make baked goods. I vowed to never work in food service or at 5 am again. Yet, I would have never discerned my desire to not work in food service without actually working in that bakery. I would have never been empowered to leave that job without being burned by a pan of biscuits. The pain of that experience helped reveal a piece of my purpose.

That day I vowed to find a job I enjoyed, not just make money. I eventually worked at two jewelry stores in college and loved it. Years later at a leadership conference, one of the speakers said, "Leaders don't need permission to lead. Innovators don't need permission to innovate." I thought to myself, yes! That is what being empowered is all about.

Myth: I must wait for permission from someone else to act.

Truth: I am empowered to act now.

Coaching Practice:

What big idea have you been waiting for permission to move forward on?

_____

_____

_____

_____

_____

_____

_____

_____

_____

What's God calling you to do next?

_____

_____

_____

_____

_____

_____

_____

_____

You've got permission now. God has created you to be innovative, creative and smart enough to do something new in the world. You have permission from God. That's all you need.

3. Make Progress not Perfection

I remember being a chubby little girl. In our culture, little girls with round shapes were called "thick." As a young girl, I had a bubbly personality and loved people. I never thought much about my body image until the eighth grade when a cute boy said, in reference to my butt as he watched me walk away, "That must be jam because jelly don't shake like that." That was the moment I became self-conscious about my round shape. Maybe you know what it feels like to be judged by others as not good enough, not smart enough, or not pretty enough.

That experience led me to exercise more and watch what I ate. It wasn't a drastic change on the outside, rather a subtle shift internally. I wanted to be healthier, stronger, and slimmer. Six months later, I lost fifteen pounds during the summer before my freshman year in high school. Today, I weigh pretty much the same as I did in high school and I know it is largely because of that one comment in the eighth grade that shifted my consciousness about myself. What started as a physical exercise was actually much more; it was spiritual. I've never had a perfect body. None of us do, because it doesn't exist. I've never lived perfectly, because that doesn't exist either. Progress is about a daily commitment to be better, do better and honor God more fully with our lives. Becoming healthier and stronger, that's progress, not perfection.

Myth: I am what others think of me. I must be perfect.

Truth: I am NOT what others think of me. I am a beautiful work in progress and have no need to be perfect.

Coaching Practice:

What are you self-critical about in your life? Your body? Your work? Your lifestyle? Your family? Describe what that feels like.

_____
_____
_____
_____
_____
_____
_____
_____
_____

Now imagine God is speaking to you about progress, not perfection. What do you hear God saying about each of the areas above in your life?

_____
_____
_____
_____
_____
_____
_____
_____

Remember, don't worry about doing every single thing exactly right in your life. Instead, love yourself and don't be too self-critical. If you can honestly say you've done your best, then you can go to bed with peace every night.

4.   Focus on Quality Not Quantity

In contemporary American society, success is often measured by hours worked, projects finished, or money acquired. Mantras such as, "just do it," "work-work-work," and "what have you done for me lately" are increasingly the norm. We hurry from place to place doing the next task so it can be checked off of our to-do list. Smart phones, tablets, laptops and TV watching also teach us to move quickly from one thought to the next. Psychiatrist Carl Jung once remarked, "Hurry is not of the Devil, it is the Devil." At the same time, I often hear people struggle with questions such as, "What is my purpose? What is my calling?" Many people are starving to death in secret while working hard. Their souls are starving from lack of a deep relationship with God. The reality is as humans we are constantly battling between our ego (mental and physical self-image) and our spiritual (or divine) image. Dr. Wayne Dyer in his book, The Power of Intention, names six ego assumptions (myths) which block us from living the higher purposes of our lives. Two of these myths are:

I am what I have. My possessions define me.

I am what I do. My achievements define me.

So how do we overcome these assumptions and the addiction to hurry? It starts with a shift from the quantity of output as the purpose of life to the quality of love and life. We may never have as much money, possessions, or achievements as we desire, but God's measure of our success is the quality of our self love and commitment to making the lives of others better.

Myths: I am what I have. My possessions define me. I am what I do. My achievements define me.

Truths: I am NOT what I have. My possessions DO NOT define me. I am NOT what I do. My achievements DO NOT define me. I am an eternal, beautiful soul having a physical experience.

Coaching Practice:

Name three things that can improve the QUALITY of your life this week. These are activities that delight and intentionally cultivate joy in your life. What specific actions can you take to work towards these improvements?

_____

_____

_____

_____

_____

_____

_____

_____

_____

_____

_____

_____

_____

_____

5. Be Courageous

Courage is what makes someone capable of facing extreme danger and difficulty without retreating, according to the New Oxford American Dictionary. It takes courage to confront challenges head-on in our everyday lives. Courage implies not only bravery or a bold spirit but also, the ability to endure in times of adversity. For example, it takes courage to simply get up when you've faced huge losses like the death of a loved one, the loss of a job, or a health challenge. How courageous are you?

Courage is also extending grace to yourself and others while under pressure. Maybe you're feeling pressure to get it all done, to be "perfect," or to be better than someone else. The truth is you are human. I'm human. We all fail sometimes. Not giving up is an act of courage. We will only succeed if we try. As you discern the future steps on your journey, make courageous choices, no matter what others think. In time, courageous decisions of faith will yield the greatest impact in your life. You are courageous.

I remember one of the first nights in our new home. Kevin and I were newly married and I had moved miles away from my family in St. Louis to start a new life in Kansas City at the age of twenty-five. We had jobs, a home, and each other, but that night I sat on the floor of the home we had just purchased and cried. I missed my family, friends, and the familiarity of my hometown. What was supposed to be a wonderful time of life felt awful. I had a choice to make. I could sulk and be miserable or I could get back up with the help of God. I realized my grief was from feeling alone and isolated. I knew I needed to make new friends if I was going to enjoy our new life. Kevin could not be my only friend. This step required me to be honest with myself, vulnerable with strangers, and take risks. It took six months, but I met new people, visited new places and have met some amazing people who have blessed my life in Kansas City. I know for sure God used my move to Kansas City and feelings of isolation to build courage within me. Actually, courage has always been there. I just needed to practice it and be reminded that I can do all things through Christ who strengthens me.

Jesus Christ, despite being beaten, attacked and humiliated on a cross to die, gave his life so that thousands of years later humanity could be free. Harriet Tubman led African American slaves to freedom on the Underground Railroad. Rosa Parks refused to give up her seat on a segregated city bus. Rev. Dr. Martin Luther King dedicated his life to a courageous nonviolent movement for civil rights. They and many others are our role models.

Myths: Fear is greater than faith. Fear often stops me. I am not a role model.

Truths: My courage is always with me. I am strong and full of courage. My courage helps inspire others to be courageous.

Coaching Practice:

Who are you when you are at your courageous best? List descriptions of yourself beginning with, I am…

_____

_____

_____

_____
_____
_____
_____
_____
_____
_____
_____
_____
_____
_____

How will you live courageously? What one new thing will you dare to try in the next seven days because of your courage?

_____
_____
_____
_____
_____
_____
_____
_____
_____
_____
_____
_____
_____

6. Claim Your Vision

When I was thirteen years old, my grandfather came to live with my family. Granddaddy Al, my father's dad, was a handsome and wise man. He wore a suit most every day, up until the last years of his life. Granddaddy left his hometown of Baton Rouge, Louisiana, at the young age of thirteen to venture out on his own. He took the train to Chicago and hustled his way forward. He was an entrepreneur, a creator of African woodcarvings, and a spiritual guide over the course of his life. Granddaddy was losing his eyesight due to diabetes when he came to live with us. Over the course of several years, his eyesight got progressively worse. He felt his way around the house. I would watch him, even though essentially blind, make his way to the bus stop to ride and visit friends. He would feel his way to produce African woodcarvings in the back yard. I was amazed at his resiliency and keen sense of continuing to move forward. Granddaddy had a vision of himself that was greater than his physical eyesight. He sensed his life's work continued well beyond what his physical eye could see.

Today, I am grateful for my physical eyesight. With the help of contacts, I have 20-20 vision. Yet, I know as soon as I take my contacts out at night my eyesight is seriously limited. Though I can see up close, my ability to peer across the room or to drive is vastly diminished. However, there is a spiritual vision that goes beyond what my eyes can see. Spiritual vision is a gift from God that's available to every person. It's a third eye that sees beyond the current situation. What do you see with your third eye? What's your vision for your life?

Myth: I can't see my future because my present is uncertain.

Truth: God provides a vision of my future that I can see despite my present situation. Through my spiritual third eye, I discover my life's purpose.

Coaching Practice:

If you had all the money and time you needed, what would you be doing?

_____

_____

_____

_____

_____

How would you help other people?

_____

_____

_____

_____

_____

How would the world be different?

_____

_____

_____

_____

_____

Remember, as my coach, Rev, Rodney Smothers, recently said, "God's provision precedes the vision." So, don't worry about how the vision will happen. Our job is to believe and courageously work towards the vision.

7.   Be Proactive not Reactive

I remember telling my dad I wanted to be a writer. He promptly said, "Writers write." Wow! What a simple, yet profound statement. It reminds me that the point of writing, or any discipline, is doing it for the love of creating and developing, whether anyone will ever read it or not. That's what being proactive is about. Proactive literally means planning for and taking intentional action. It's choosing how you want to move forward, despite what others think or say and taking responsibility for our own happiness. The opposite of proactive is reactive. Reactive means responding to an external source, such as someone else's request. While there are times we all choose to respond to other's needs and our faith calls us to help people, routinely choosing to put other's needs before our own is not powerful. It diminishes our joy and depletes our energy.

Author Steven R. Covey in his book, The 7 Habits of Highly Effective People, reminds us that contrary to popular belief "Your life doesn't just happen." Whether you know it or not, it is carefully designed by you. The choices, after all, are yours. You choose happiness. You choose sadness. You choose decisiveness. You choose ambivalence. You choose success. You choose failure. You choose courage. You choose fear. Just remember that every moment, every situation, provides a new choice. And in doing so, it gives you a perfect opportunity to do things differently to produce more positive results."

Myths: I can't. I have to. I don't have a choice.

Truth: I can. I will. I am free to choose.

Coaching Practice:

How will you choose to live proactively? Describe the shifts you'd like to make beginning this week. For example, how can you use proactive language?

_____
_____
_____
_____
_____
_____
_____
_____
_____
_____

Pray the following Serenity Prayer each day this week as you speak and live proactively.

God, grant me the serenity to accept the things I cannot change, courage to change the things I can, and wisdom to know the difference.

By Reinhold Niebuhr, American theologian (1892–1971)

8. Keep Hope Alive

On Wednesday, November 9, 2016, I woke up to the news that Donald Trump had been elected as the 45th president of the United States of America. While he lost the popular vote by more than three million votes, he secured the necessary electoral votes to win. This election follows eight years of Barack Obama's presidency that was filled with hope for many Americans, including myself. Not only was he the first African American president, he led the country through the 2008 economic crisis and led the efforts to secure universal health care insurance for all Americans. His presidency was filled with progress, optimism, and an expectation that the best of times were still to come for our country and its citizens. Yet, on November 9, I felt as if the hope I had in my country and fellow Americans was shattered with the election of Trump.

How do we, as people of faith, respond when what we hoped for doesn't happen? One strategy for me lies in the image of a twice-baked potato. The first baking of the potato is the base. It's the first step but not the final product. The yumminess of the twice-baked potato comes only after the cooked inside of the potato is scooped out, mixed with other ingredients like butter, bacon and sour cream and put back into the shell for baking again. Likewise, think about our hopes and dreams as needing to be baked twice. First, there is the mental and spiritual creation of what we hope for in our head and hearts. Second is the physical manifestation. Sometimes the outcome looks like what we expected, other times not. What we create today in our hearts and minds will impact what happens in the future. So, we keep hope alive until the love, joy, and goodness we imagine actually happens. Our work is to be proactive in creating love, joy, and goodness twice and the world will be a better place.

Myth: Hope is loss when things don't work out the way I expected.

Truth: I am filled with hope no matter what.

Coaching Practice:

Let's practice active hope in our personal, professional, and community life. Just like writing, gardening, or playing sports, it is something we do rather than have. Here's a quick three-step process to help us practice. Fill in the grid below using these steps. First, describe the current reality in an area of your personal, professional, or community life. Next, identify what you hope for. Finally, identify one step you can take towards that hope. Ready. Set. Go.

	Current reality is…	What I hope for…	Step to get there…
My Health			
My Relationships			
My Finances			
My Community/ Church			

9. Know Your Story

Today, I find myself looking into a mirror and asking, "Who am I?" In the mirror, I see an African American woman, mother, wife, sister, and friend living in a suburb of Kansas City, Missouri. I grew up in St. Louis with my parents and one brother. I attended college and graduate school for business in Missouri. I met my husband while in college. Based on the U.S. Census Bureau data pertaining to income and education, we are upper-middle class, yet my friends and family span all social classes, races, genders, sexual orientations, and physical abilities. Growing up in diverse social situations, I learned the importance of family, discipline, education, responsibility, acceptance, and faith.

At an early age, my parents shared stories of slavery, segregation, and civil rights in the U.S. with me. My mother's family migrated from Philadelphia, Mississippi (Neshoba County) in the 1960's to St. Louis and brought with them many stories of injustices against blacks. For example, my second cousin was severely beaten by whites for walking down the street with his light-skinned black cousin, who they thought was white, while he was black. In June 1964, the infamous three civil rights workers were abducted and murdered in an act of racial violence as they attempted to register African Americans to vote during the "Freedom Summer" campaign. This was only fifty years ago in my mother's hometown. This feels strangely recent to me.

My father was also very active in the civil rights struggle of the 1960's. As a student on a predominately-white college campus in Kirksville, Missouri, he was instrumental in the racial integration of restaurants as he led several sit-ins at lunch counters with the local Methodist minister. He was active in the young Democrats club and went on to become a college history professor and an attorney.

The stories, symbols and images my parents shared shaped my understanding of my identity as an American. While we lived comfortably in the suburbs of St. Louis where my brother and I attended private Christian schools, I gained a deep sense of my responsibility to know, respect and help others, especially African Americans and others who are disadvantaged. As an adult I have lived, worked, and built friendships across race, class, age and gender.

Everyone has a past. We live in the present. And, we have the opportunity to co-create our future legacy with God. One of the mistakes we often make is believing our past doesn't matter. Contrary to popular belief, embracing your family, your history and life's experience is a key to creating the future you desire. Think of yourself for a moment as a rubber band. Rubber bands, like people, come in different sizes and experience being stretched in good and challenging ways. Even when stretched, rubber bands spring back because they are durable. Likewise, people become stronger after being stretched. One of the ways we learn to be resilient is remembering our family's story of resilience. When we recall how our foremothers and forefathers persevered through struggle, we realize we also are naturally filled with confidence, flexibility, and hope.

Growing up, my mother, "Mama," was nothing short of amazing. She birthed two children into the world, comforted my brother and I when we were sick, worked a full-time job, cooked dinner every night, and taught me the essence of unconditional love. Mama gave birth to my brother, Anthony and I during her college career. Although I was too young to remember the particulars of her pursuit of higher education, I remember her always keeping us close by as she journeyed toward her goal. Years later, she shared stories of late night studying, editing of her research papers by my dad, and her perseverance to get a college degree. She was full of limitless determination. She often said, "You gotta get an education to make it in this world." It is no coincidence that today both my brother and I have masters degrees and prod our own children toward academic excellence. God chose Mama to be my first teacher. As Dr. Marian Wright Edelman says in her book Lanterns, "I do what I do because my parents did what they did and were who they were. I first saw God's face in the face of my parents and heard God's voice in theirs as they cooed, read, told stories, and sang to me."

As a young adult, I can remember when I realized my mother had also become my friend. I was away from home in a new city, newly engaged to be married. It felt as if I had no friends or support group. During this time, I found immense comfort knowing I could call my mother, anytime day or night when I was troubled or to share joys, like finding a new friend. She listened, provided words of comfort, and calmed my worries just as she did rocking me when I was a child. Today, we have a covenant of caring and trust.

Myth: Forget the past. Just move forward.

Truth: Honoring my past helps strengthen my future.

Coaching Practice:

Take time to interview your parents or close family relatives to discover more about your family DNA using the questions below. Listen to their stories. Ask open-ended questions and listen for the emotions behind the stories. Audio or video record the interviews if possible, so you'll have a record for your keeping. Start by answering these questions for yourself.

What's your earliest memory of your family life? What lessons did you learn?

_____

_____

_____

_____

_____

Describe the best memory from your teen years? What did you learn about yourself?

_____

_____

_____

_____

_____

As you look back over your life what threads do you recognize? What sacred truths come to mind?

_____

_____

_____

10. Redefine Success

In everything he did he had great success, because the LORD was with him (1 Samuel 18:14, NIV).

January 2008, it was a Tuesday afternoon in South Africa, the last day of summer vacation for school children and their families. The temperature was unseasonably cool for summer time, yet people were swimming in the Atlantic Ocean and children played outside. A few miles away from the baby blue water and fine beach homes lay a local township of black Africans named Masiphumelele, which means "We Have Succeeded." Ms. Charlotte, our tour guide, a Masiphumelele resident, smiled widely and welcomed us to the community of approximately 22,000 people. Most of the homes in this township were "tin shacks" by western standards. Few people had cars. Approximately 60% of the people were without jobs and 42% were afflicted with HIV/AIDS according to Ms. Charlotte. At first glance, I was baffled when Ms. Charlotte said, "We are blessed." This experience begged me to ask, "What is success?" In our western culture, success is often defined by bank accounts, BMWs and bling. If this definition was accurate, how could 22,000 people living in poverty, joblessness, and sickness be successful? I wondered how God defined success. In 1 Samuel 18:14, David's success was based on God's presence with him in the face of his enemies. This success had little to do with material possessions. Success in the Hebrew Bible often means "to rise up" or "to be wise." As people of God, we are called to spread a message of success as demonstrated in Masiphumelele which is more merciful than materialistic, more loving than lustful, and more communal than individual. So today, we celebrate the blessings and challenges of the people of Masiphumelele and proclaim, "We Have Succeeded!"

Myth: Success is defined by my bank account, title, and status.

Truth: With God, I am successful despite any circumstance.

Coaching Practice:

Define success for your life. How will you know when you've been successful? Whose life will you make better?

_____
_____
_____
_____
_____

How will you use your gifts and talents to bless others this week?

_____
_____
_____
_____
_____

Prayer: God, we thank you for the beautiful spirit of the people of Masiphumelele. We pray that the work you have begun in all of South Africa of love, empowerment and forgiveness prospers. Help us to always remember the lessons of the people as we challenge ourselves to redefine success by your standards. In Jesus name we pray. Amen

Part II: Explore

How to cultivate a life that RISES?

I remember as a little girl going outside to play and searching the neighborhood for other children along with my brother, Anthony, to play with. Playtime was always more fun with a group. We would play tag, ride skateboards, race on our bikes, or play jump rope. Do you remember those days? What was your favorite game? Who did you play it with? Children thrive on gathering together for fun, whether it's recess during the school day or in playing in the neighborhood on the weekends. Children thrive through connection with one another. Yet, somewhere along the way, as adults, we buy into the myth of individualism. We begin to compete instead of collaborate, thinking in terms of scarcity of resources, recognition and accomplishment instead of abundance.

To live out our purpose in life and become the who God empowers us to be requires that we gather with others of like mind, heart and purpose. Who will be on your journey with you on your team? And, whose team will you be on?

I've always enjoyed team sports. There's something deeply satisfying about practicing, persevering, and winning together as a team. Our two sons, Isaac and Aaron play competitive baseball. While there are individual moments of batting or pitching, baseball is a team sport. It requires collaboration and commitment to cultivate a great baseball team like the 2015 Kansas City Royals who won the World Series. Go Royals!

The word cultivation is often used to describe how gardeners take care of crops. However, in a more general sense, the verb cultivate means to improve, practice, or train someone or something. Athletes cultivate their skills through practice. Writers cultivate skills by writing. Importantly, we don't develop these skills alone. We grow by practicing as a team. For women deep at the heart of cultivation is a commitment to sisterhood. I grew up as the only daughter of my parents. So while I never had biological sisters, I have been surrounded by a wonderful group of friends and family who are my sisters. Who are the sisters God is calling you to work with to achieve your dream? It is a myth that we accomplish greatness alone. Greatness is cultivated together.

The following principles in Part 2 of this book are based on the assumption that practice of any skill with others can be transformative. Practices purposely planned and designed can revolutionize our perception of ourselves and our capacity to move forward powerfully as warrior chicks. You will see themes of teamwork, collaboration, commitment, and cultivation. Each concept challenges a myth and replaces it with a truth. Embracing, living and sharing these truths will free us to pursue what really matters. They will enable us to live at our highest level of purpose, vision and joy. Finally, at the end of each truth are coaching exercises and questions to support you in cultivating your life as she who rises.

11.   Welcome Transitions
12.   Build Your Team
13.   Trust Your Gut
14.   Choose Your Words Carefully

15. Name the Divine; She is God
16. Practice Breathing & Meditation
17. Listen To Your Voice
18. Begin Passion Planning
19. Get a Coach
20. Teach What You're Learning

11. Welcome Transitions

One morning, I journeyed through the rituals of shepherding our kids to the bus stop, rushing to preschool drop off, and finally grabbing my morning coffee. On the outside it was just another rainy spring morning, but on the inside something felt unusual, unfamiliar, and unsettling. Perhaps you've felt this way before. It's a feeling that often arises in-between times. It's the space between an ending and a new beginning, between grief and joy, between despair and hope. I felt this way when I moved from St. Louis to Kansas City, transitioned from corporate America to ministry, and from being without children to motherhood.

We all go through transitions in life that feel unusual, unfamiliar, and cause an unsettling of our souls. Change is a part of life. But, we do have a choice in HOW we live through these times. This particular day, was one of the last days I would be a pastor of the church I founded. I was transitioning from pastoral ministry to coaching and non-profit leadership. While I knew this was a call by God, this time of transition required me to honor the past, open my heart towards the future, and remember my strengths. Oh, and guess what? That rainy spring morning turned into a sunny afternoon that was beautiful!

The Apostle Paul declared in Romans 8:38-39, "We are afflicted in every way, but not crushed; perplexed, but not driven to despair; persecuted, but not forsaken; struck down, but not destroyed..." I love the way Paul acknowledges his feelings, but then declares hope.

Myth: Transitions make me weak.

Truth: Transitions make me stronger and are a path towards success.

Coaching Practice:

Here are five ways I move through transitions with hope. Practice one of these strategies this week.

1. Slow down. Instead of rushing, intentionally create more margin in your schedule to savor each day.

2. Look small. Instead of worrying about the future, look for small gifts like hearing the birds chirp, smelling the rain, and watching the sunrise from behind the clouds.

3. Dance in the rain. In the moments when you don't feel like dancing, intentionally turn on an upbeat song and dance like nobody is watching.

4. Find support at this helpful website titled Liminal Space...Finding Life Between Chapters. Check it out at http://inaliminalspace.com.

5. Remember your strengths using the Strengths Finder assessment. Check out http://strengths.gallup.com for more details on how to discover your strengths. I've learned my top strengths are as follows.

1. *Learner* - I love to learn. What interests me most is leadership, personal development, marketing, and spirituality. The process of seeking out new information, more than the content or the result, is especially exciting for me. I'm energized by the intentional journey from not knowing to an "aha" moment of knowing something new and connecting it to questions about life and people. The excitement of learning leads me to spend lots of time at the library exploring and reading

new books. I also embrace new experiences like yoga, meditation, and riding the hover board our boys got for Christmas. How about you? What do you love to learn?

2. *Relator* - Relationships are important to me. As a relator, I'm selective about my close relationships, but I enjoy a large network of acquaintances. I enjoy investing in a few deeper relationships. This strength has led me to the profession of coaching. As a coach, I have the joy of working with people to improve leadership skills, communication skills, and better manage stress and change. I help people improve their quality of life and happiness in their career, community, family, spirituality, and overall well-being. This is a way I live out my calling.

3. *Achiever* - I am driven. As an achiever, I have a constant need for achievement and every day starts at zero. By the end of the day, I must achieve something tangible in order to feel good about the day, no matter how small. I have an internal fire burning inside me that pushes me to do more, to achieve more. After each accomplishment is reached, the fire dwindles, but within twenty-four hours, it's back and ready to go. As an achiever, I've learned to live with this whisper of discontent and still be at peace. My natural drive brings the energy I need to work long hours, take on new challenges, and keeps me moving forward.

4. *Maximizer* - As a maximizer, excellence, not average, is my goal. Taking something from good to great excites me. I want to see people live their best life and nothing less. I find myself naturally encouraging people to capitalize on the gifts with which they are blessed, to soar and achieve greatness. This is the life that's more fun. It's more productive. And, while it takes effort,

maximizing our gifts is what brings deep satisfaction in life individually and collectively. Striving towards excellence as a team, achieving success, and celebrating together is awe-inspiring.

5. *Activator* - "Let's go!" This is a recurring axiom in my life. Admittedly, I am impatient for action. I believe in analysis, discussion, and planning, but deep down I know only action is real. Only action can make things happen. Only action leads to success. Importantly, I believe action or practice is the best way to learn. I make a decision, take action, look at the result, and learn. There is no failure in taking action, only learning and growing. This learning informs the next step, future options, and builds courage. The bottom line is this, "People may not remember what you say, but they will always remember what you do." I posted this quote in my college dorm room and found it to be an invaluable roommate when I was overwhelmed.

List Your Top 5 Strengths Here

How can you apply these strengths to your life today?

	Strength	Application
1		
2		
3		
4		
5		

12. Build Your Team

Throughout our life's journey we meet people along the way. Some become our friends, others become acquaintances, and some are quickly gone. However, we are all impacted by the people we meet. Look at your circle of friends and acquaintances. Think of the ones closest to you. Maybe you have the same interests, hobbies or values. Maybe your children are friends and you have play dates, which bring you together. Some you've met in school and shared significant life moments. We are all created for relationship. We need each other and God has made us to depend on one another. Now, imagine cultivating a group of likeminded people with shared values and dreams who all joined forces to make a "great thing" happen. Imagine the movement and force behind the energy of a group of people versus one person going it alone. This is the essence of team building. Momentum happens with a critical mass of people committed to the same goal. Imagine this momentum is like a snowball. Once the snowball starts moving, it moves forward powerfully and can rarely be stopped.

Some of us have been taught it is only wise to depend on yourself and never look to anyone for help. I've heard countless times during my life that we must be strong and independent. But, there is also another saying, "Work smarter, not harder." Collaboration and team building are key elements to being successful in life. No one person knows everything, but many people know many things. Look to your friends you have "gathered" over the years. They're waiting to share their resources, knowledge, and skills with you and you can do the same for them.

Myth: I can only depend on myself. I never look to anyone for help.

Truth: I am created for collaboration and to accomplish greatness with a team.

Coaching Practice:

To achieve any significant goal requires a support team with at least six essential people. And, the bigger the dream the more important these people are. Take a moment to write down the names of twelve people (two in each area) who could support you in each of these areas. Everyone has different gifts and talents. Remember to build on your strengths and invite people to your team who have different strengths than yours.

Six Team Members Every Dreamer Needs

1) Someone who believes in you no matter what and will encourage you along the way.

_____

_____

_____

2) Someone with expertise in the area of your goal. Remember you don't have to be the expert, but you will need support and coaching from someone who is.

_____

_____

_____

3) Someone with finance experience. Your dream will need to be funded.

_____

_____

_____

4) Someone with online marketing experience. You'll need to spread your message online.

_____

_____

_____

5) An expert communicator. People exceptionally talented in communication find it easy to put thoughts into words. They are good conversationalists and presenters.

_____

_____

_____

6) Someone with Woo. People exceptionally talented in the Woo theme love the challenge of meeting new people and winning them over. They derive satisfaction from breaking the ice and making a connection with someone.

_____

_____

_____

By when will you contact each person and ask for their support via email or phone? List the dates next to each name above.

13.   Learn to Trust Your Gut

I was a good student, all throughout school. I worked hard to get good grades because I loved the feeling of achievement. I always wanted to be the smartest in the class. I carefully read the directions for each assignment, completed each part methodically, and checked the answers twice. I was eager to get A's and be affirmed for my intellect. Even today I love writing lists and checking items off at the end of the day.

In college, I was intrigued by math and poured myself into the business curriculum. I loved marketing and learning how people made decisions. I read my assignments three times, took notes, and could regurgitate the business philosophies my professors taught. I treasured my study time and was exceptionally committed to being a great student. I graduated in the top 10% of my class, magna cum laude.

This strong work ethic also helped me excel as a marketing manager in corporate America.

Yet, after toiling for twelve years and being promoted every two years on average, I questioned whether the promotions, titles, rewards, power and opportunities were worth the cost. My feelings of restlessness were signs for me to pay attention. This was the beginning of learning to trust my own gut and the messages deep within my soul.

One day during this restless season, I received an invitation to visit Saint Paul School of Theology. Out of nowhere, it seemed I was intrigued enough to visit the school. That day I went home with the resolve to take a deeper journey into my faith and to pursue a Master's of Divinity degree. Sometime later, I embraced my unusual vocation as a minister. I would have never predicted this would be the course of my life.

All this happened ten years ago. During seminary, I slowly learned to trust my own thoughts and feelings and to first look inside myself for wisdom. I began to write, not just regurgitate what others said. I discovered my own voice. Here's an excerpt from my early writing journey in seminary.

Writing is my work. I am called to hone this craft to somehow build the kingdom, share wisdom, and carry on stories so future generations will benefit from what God says to me. I let go of all my fears...what if it's not good...what if no one reads it...it does not matter...I will still write. I will learn the craft, practice the craft, and share it with others. Writing is liberation! Writing is like the very air I breathe. Listening is part of what makes this possible. I will listen with my heart. I will appreciate others and what they have to offer knowing that we are all children of God. God, have your way with me. I thank you for my sisters and foremothers that have walked this path before me and for Dr. Simms who is now choosing to sow into me. I thank you, Lord! I have greatness on the inside of me that will now be loosed! I am ready to become who you have called me to be. I am, therefore I write. I am, therefore I listen with my heart. I am, therefore I sow forward in all that I do. I do the hard stuff and celebrate along the way. Will it be easy? No. Will it be worth it? Absolutely. I want to make you proud, God. I love you, Lord. I worship you with my writing.

Communicating is a gift. Whether you write, speak, dance, sing, or draw, feel the connection of your movement to the heart. Experiment knowing that your inside world creates the outside world. And, your outside world, tools, and environment also impact your thoughts.

Myth: Wisdom comes from knowing what other say.

Truth: Wisdom first comes from within and is stimulated from engagement with the outside world.

Coaching Practice:

What is your gut saying to you? How are you uniquely being called forth? What makes you stand out? Take the next five-minutes to free write. Trust your first thoughts. Keep your hand moving. Don't cross out. Don't make corrections. Don't think. Speak truth. Just write.

_____

_____

_____

_____

_____

_____

_____

_____

_____

_____

_____

_____

14. Choose Your Words Carefully

As a young girl I learned the words, "Sticks and stones may break my bones, but words will never hurt." That was a lie. The words we use to describe ourselves, others, and God shape our sense of identity and thus our destiny. What do you say about yourself? Do you describe yourself most often in positive or negative terms? We must continually define and redefine our language for ourselves instead of letting others do it for us. Words can either build up or tear down. One of the times I first intently thought about my words is when I became a mother of our first son, Isaac. Instinctively, without my conscious thought, the words I spoke mattered so much more. One of the words I contemplated the most after conceiving and birthing Isaac was "motherhood." I immediately had a new identity. But nurturing, caring, supporting, and loving a child was all new. In the words of Kristen Clark Taylor, "At every child's birth, a mother is born." Yet, embracing the mother within me took several weeks and months as I waded through postpartum depression. Eventually, with the support of loving and wise women, I realized mothering happens by a village of friends, relatives and neighbors, and I asked for help.

Another word I often contemplate is "woman." In particular, what does it mean to be a black woman in the United States? To answer this question, I fervently studied the history of slavery in the United States and how it impacted black women. As early as 1619 and through the mid-nineteenth century, between ten and eleven million Africans were enslaved. Slavery had a devastating impact on the culture of the African family and on the identity of black women. Within slavery, black women played many roles including that of "field hand," "mammy," and "breeder." These forced roles were possible because slaves did not own their bodies or their manual labor. Delores Williams writes, "Her body, like her labor, could be exploited in any way her owners desired." In this quote, Williams is talking about the slave Hagar in the Bible (Genesis, chapter 16), but her point is applicable to black women enslaved in the U.S. Women were property of their slave owners and were often taken away from their own families and forced to support the slave owner's family. Their service was exploited in any way the owner deemed necessary including grinding manual labor, demeaning domestic duties, and humiliating sexual exploitation.

Most black women in the U.S. during the time of slavery worked in the fields, labored the same number of hours as men, and were dominated and tyrannized just as men were for the profit of the slave owner. Women worked side by side with men in the fields planting, cultivating and harvesting crops such as rice, corn, sugar and cotton. Even when women were pregnant, they were expected to work the same number of hours in the fields. Unity existed between women and men because they had a common goal of surviving slavery and having some quality of life for themselves and their families. There was mutual respect, camaraderie and compassion among women and men. In contrast, the patriarchal and capitalistic plantation economy devalued black women and diminished their womanhood. For example, black women were accused of having an "aggressive nature" and thus not meeting the ideal of a submissive wife and mother. The assertive nature that was required to be successful in fieldwork was used to undermine and devalue black women.

Mammies worked as house servants doing domestic work such as cooking, cleaning and taking care of the slave owner's children. This role was typically found only in the homes of wealthy slave owners, but was more common during post-slavery times in the first half of the twentieth century. The mammy epitome is "the black woman, like 'Aunt Jemima', who is very dark in color, fat, nurturing, kind, religious, and strong." In other words, mammy was created to be ugly and physically opposite to the ideal white woman who was very light in skin color and thinner. Importantly, mammy had to manage the household well, while always being faithful to "honor the power of the slave master and his wife." In other words, like women who worked in the field, the drudgery of the mammy inside the master's house was also under the strict control of the white family.

Breeders were African American women slaves who were forced to have sexual relations with any man the slave owner provided, including himself, to birth children who would become slaves. The black woman as a breeder further illustrates the patriarchal power that white slave masters had over black women slaves. Delores Williams writes, "During slavery, breeder women were mated with any male the slaveholder chose so that the women could give birth every twelve months. These children would become the property of the slaveholder. If the white slave holder could not find a mate he deemed adequate for mating with the 'breeder woman,' he would mate with her himself.

Slave women were mated with a 'stud,' just as race horses are today and for the same reason—profit."

In other words, black women's bodies since the inception of chattel slavery have been abused as the property of another.

So, the question for you and I is, "What we will say about ourselves?" Beyond our history, which is admittedly horrific for black women, we are survivors, worthy of love. We are women and mothers who are nurturing, caring, supporting, and loving all of God's creation. Beyond all, we still rise. Will the words we say about ourselves, to ourselves, and about one another as women be empowering, uplifting and loving or defeating, degrading or hateful?

Myth: Black women are field hands, mammies, and breeders.

Truth: Black women are beautiful, survivors, and worthy of love.

Coaching Practice:

List ten uplifting words that describe you and other women. Begin to use these in your speech to uplift one another starting today.

_____
_____
_____
_____
_____
_____

As an affirmation of all women celebrate by reciting this poem titled *Still I Rise* by Maya Angelou.

Out of the huts of history's shame, I rise

Up from a past that's rooted in pain, I rise;

I'm a black ocean, leaping and wide;

Welling and swelling I bear in the tide.

Leaving behind nights of terror and fear, I rise;

Into a daybreak that's wondrously clear, I rise;

Bringing the gifts that my ancestors gave,

I am the dream and the hope of the slave.

I rise, I rise, I rise.

15.   Name the Divine; She is God

As a young girl, I remember learning to pray before dinner saying, "God is great. God is good. Let us thank him for our food. Amen." I became an expert at quickly reciting this prayer so I could dive into my favorite foods like tacos, pizza and Mama's hamburger casserole. Yet, I never once stopped and contemplated, "Who is God?" Even as an adult who attended church on most Sundays, I recited the Lord's Prayer saying, "Our Father which art in heaven..." without questioning the metaphor of God as Father. Today, I wrestle with the question, "Who is the spirit we name God?"

A name is hardly ever just a random label. For example, when contemplating the names of our children, Kevin and I poured over baby books, talked to friends and even listened to music for possible names. We considered the origin, biblical meaning, cultural significance, popularity, and even the strength of many names. Names have meaning and often communicate the essence of what a thing is. Indian Jesuit theologian, Samuel Rayan writes, "The fact that at times people change their names (as do monks and nuns, popes, etc.) is proof indeed that names matter and have links with life and its meanings." In other words, naming is power. Power in this sense is not dominance, but rather influence to shape meaning.

How we name the world shapes the world. For example, what we name as good becomes valued. What we name as bad, becomes devalued. In religious life, whatever one names God ascribes particular attributes to God. Naming God also assigns value or power to particular human attributes, functions and interactions.

For example, if God is father then acts of fathering and males are of supreme value to God and endowed with power from God. Yet, what if God is mother? What if God is "she" instead of just "he"?

The importance of naming God cannot be underestimated for women. Historically in the U.S. and across the globe, women have been powerless to name God. Naming God as she and mother is a way for all women to reclaim the goodness of femaleness, nurturing, wisdom, roundness of hips, and voice in the world. Feminist theologian, Elizabeth Johnson speaks of God as "She Who Is" or one who goes beyond our human boundaries, yet is in mutual relationship with all of creation who dwells within her.

We must acknowledge that while conceiving and naming God in our own image can make God present with us, God also transcends our human understanding. In other words, She is both with us, shapes us, and is more than us.

Myth: God is only father. He can only be imagined as male.

Truth: God is also mother. She who is God is with us.

Coaching Practice:

Describe who God is as a woman and mother in your own words.

_____

_____

_____

_____

As an affirmation of all women and God as mother celebrate by praying this prayer today.

God as Mother/Mama: "Love and Light" Ps. 27

By Lia McIntosh

In the midst of a busy day, your love is my light of hope. Your joy and reassurance is my peace. Your love and light calms my spirit and nourishes my soul. Your love and light show me where to go. When nothing else works I can count on, lean on, and press on because of your light and love.

Mama, God, let your light shine today in a supernatural way that everyone who sees you will have faces that smile, hearts that rejoice, legs that dance, toes that tap, and eyes that flutter with the revelation of your Mother love.

May our souls rest, fears calm, and backs straighten because of your light and love, dear Mama. Amen.

16. Practice Breathing & Meditation

I first learned to really breathe during childbirth classes. As a first time mom, I had no idea what contractions would feel like. The nurse teaching the class at our local hospital taught us "patterned breathing." It is the practice of switching between deep breathing and light breathing to relax the body and mind when pain comes. In the midst of hours of labor, I got lots of practice breathing. Since then, I've learned to breathe my way through pain, stress, and uncertainty in everyday life. It has especially brought calm, rest, reassurance, and an experience of God's presence when combined with meditation.

What is meditation? There are many definitions. The dictionary defines meditation as, "continued or extended thought, reflection, or contemplation; devout religious contemplation or spiritual introspection." Richard J. Foster, a contemporary writer and speaker on Christian spirituality, defines Christian meditation as "a 'portable sanctuary,' an inward fellowship that transfers the inner personality whereby our desires and aspirations are more conformed to righteousness and peace and joy." James Finley, a former monk and leading contemporary writer and speaker on meditation, defines it as, "an act of religious faith; a journey of learning to be in union with God; a place of refuge and transformation." Donald K. McKim, author of the Westminster Dictionary of Theological Terms, writes that meditation comes from the Latin word meditatio which means "a thinking over"; it is "reflection and thought upon a subject, often a scriptural passage, and often coupled with prayer, as an exercise in Christian devotion in order to gain spiritual insight."

For me, meditation is simply the awareness of God's presence all around and within whether in the sanctuary, shower, or at work. It is being attentive, open and receptive to God's Spirit with every breath we take. It is peace, joy and love.

So, what is meditation not? It is not complicated and it does not require any special spiritual gifts or experience. Meditation is as natural as the first breath of the morning and last of the evening. It is an encounter with God.

In Matthew 11:28-30, Jesus called everyone to "Come to me, all you who are weary and burdened, and I will give you rest. Take my yoke upon you and learn from me, for I am gentle and humble in heart, and you will find rest for your souls. For my yoke is easy and my burden is light." Jesus calls us to leave self behind, to shed materialistic stress and anxiety, to find the 'rest' of contemplation in accepting his yoke. Rest that the soul experiences through meditation makes all yokes easy, all burdens light. Meditation also enables us to do our life's work more effectively. Jesus defended the contemplative dimension of life in the story of Martha and Mary in Luke 10:38-42. In this story, Jesus commends leaving everything aside for a time to be in the presence of God. This is a life of meditation. Martha and Mary are sisters, two opposite dimensions of the person. Without Mary's laying aside of "things" and sitting at the feet of the teacher and listening, we become like Martha, irritable, complaining, discontented, distracted. In the end, we are less productive in the work we do despite thinking we are doing more. Both Mary and Martha are working, one on the internal self, the other on external things. Meditation is not an escape from one's work. It is a part of our work and helps us to do the other part better. Mary and Martha are like two chambers of one heart. They don't just complement one another; they need each other to realize fullness of life. Meditation draws us closer to God, provides rest, and enables us to do our life's work more effectively.

Myth: I am too busy to meditate.

Truth: Meditation and breathing provide calm, rest, reassurance, and an experience of God's presence. I am too busy not to meditate.

Coaching Practice:

Let's practice breathing and meditation for five minutes. Set your timer. Close your eyes. Relax right where you are and simply pay attention to your present experience in silence and stillness. Allow yourself to be, just as you are, without needing to change anything. Just focus on your breathing. Notice the feelings of breathing in and out through your nose and mouth. With each breath, relax more deeply into stillness. Simply be. If it's helpful, repeat a simple phrase in your mind such as "in, out" or "Come, Holy Spirit." Whatever thoughts or feelings arise in your mind or body, notice them, let them go, and turn your focus back to just being. Rest in peace. You are complete and whole, just as you are. When the five minutes is complete, open your eyes and slowly resume your day feeling more relaxed and centered. Remember, meditation is not any single act. It is a way of life and being.

This week set a weekly goal to meditate at least once per day for five minutes using the technique above or the ones below:

-Meditate upon scripture by letting the words slowly seep into your soul.

-Meditate upon creation. Just sit in nature and behold God's beauty.

-Meditate upon current events and ask God for guidance and discernment.

17. Listen to the Voice

I was a year out of college in 1995, had my own apartment, and was pretty content with my life. I went to church sometimes, but it wasn't the number one or number two priority in my life. Attending the church where I grew up was often boring. Yet, God spoke to me (not out loud, but clearly in my mind) and said, "GO TO CHURCH." Regardless of who will be there preaching or worshipping, I want you to be there. I grudgingly obeyed. Three years later, newly married, living in Kansas City, I started attending church with Kevin and his family. It was filled with people, great music, and vibrancy. It was the place to be for young professionals on Sunday morning. I did not want to miss the social hour. Little did I know God was working on my heart. God said to me yet again, "GO TO CHURCH." He also said, "AND LEARN MY WORD." I obeyed. It started with a Sunday school class for young adults, then a deeper bible study. It continued as I served on the usher board and as the church council secretary. Years after that first "GO TO CHURCH" encounter with God, on a Wednesday night, March 2004, I was asked to preach my first sermon. God began to reveal a vision for my life through these experiences. While I was still going through an internal time of transformation, God called me to stand out. I was not ready. I had no intention of going public with my faith. I did not fully understand what was happening. Some questioned my call and wondered if it was wise. All I knew was to follow God's leading to use my gifts and talents, one day at a time.

Now, thirteen years later, I am honored to serve the church and community as a preacher, coach, writer, strategist, community organizer, and ordained United

Methodist elder. I am an International Coaching Federation (ICF) certified Coach. As a writer, I've contributed to The Upper Room Devotional, The Abingdon Preaching Annual, and the Circuit Rider magazine. And, this work marks my first published book. I share these details to remind you that you also are gifted, talented, and ready to soar. God is speaking. Are you listening?

Myth: Nice girls don't stand out. They are seen, but not heard. Play it safe.

Truth: I am created to stand out, be seen and heard, and use my talents and gifts to help others.

Coaching Practice:

What makes you stand out? Take five minutes to journal what God is saying to you about the next step in your life. Just write from your heart. Don't edit it. Be honest. Don't hold back.

_____

_____

_____

_____

_____

_____

_____

_____

_____

_____

18. Begin Passion Planning

I was working sixty plus hours a week, leading, preaching, teaching, coaching and community organizing with three young children at home. By the end of each day, I was mentally drained, physically tired and spiritually deprived. These were the feelings that spiraled me into a strange, malaise and the problem I want to help others overcome.

I needed a tool that helped me clearly define my personal goals and dreams and put them at the forefront of my attention every day. The Passion Planner, suggested by my leadership coach, was the solution. My Passion Planner helps me break down my long and short terms goals into actionable steps and helps me incorporate each step into my daily life. It serves as a compass and accountability partner to guide my daily decisions. I ask myself: Are my plans for today going to get me closer to my goals? Yes? Do it. No? Don't do it. I know that's easier said than done. I still struggle each day with yes and no decisions. A popular TED speaker, Derek Sivers describes a simple but radical technique for becoming more selective in the choices we make. He suggests putting the decision to an extreme test. If we feel total and utter conviction to do something, then we say, "YES!" Anything less gets a thumbs down. It's either HELL YEAH! Or No. It's about learning to trust our gut reactions. Now that's freedom.

One of the things I love about the Passion Planner is that by writing everything down it helps calm my chaotic mind. Sunday night or Monday morning, I take some time to define my weekly and daily focuses. Going into the week/day with a clear goal is the best way to be productive. Admittedly, I don't practice this perfectly, but the days I do are more creative, fulfilling and peaceful.

Next, I love the Passion Roadmap. It's a place to visually see my lifetime, five year, three year and one year dreams. It's a roadmap to help me plan to do the things I'm really passionate about, like this book, not what I "should" be doing. Once my roadmap is set up at the beginning of the year, steps are created with deadlines. This translates into monthly and weekly focuses.

See images and details at http://www.passionplanner.com.

Myth: I'm too busy to plan.

Truth: By failing to prepare, you are preparing to fail.

- Benjamin Franklin

Coaching Practice:

Order your Passion Planner today at http://www.passionplanner.com.

Remember, preparation is the key to success. This week, spend fifteen minutes at the end of each day preparing for the following day using your planner. Define your "Today's Focus" and block out time to work towards your most important goals and don't forget time for yourself.

19. Get a Coach

Running has been a part of our family's daily practice all my life. Before school, we ran two to three miles most mornings. During track and cross-country season, we trained twice a day. My earliest memories of running are at seven years old when I ran my first mile "to the corner and back" through the streets of our neighborhood with my brother and dad. My father was an avid runner through high school and college. As an adult, he trained daily and ran marathons. My dad was my first coach. He coached our summer track team, studied training techniques, and pushed us to do our very best. His coaching was one of the greatest gifts of my childhood.

Today, following in my dad's footsteps, I am an ICF certified coach (http://www.coachfederation.org) that helps leaders and organizations grow. Professional coaching is similar to that of an athlete agreeing to be coached. A coach will provide the tools and structure for the athlete to make incremental or even significant changes. The athlete gives permission to the coach to be demanding because the goal for the athlete is significant and large. The athlete says, "I believe in this goal. Hold me accountable. Challenge me to do my best. Challenge me to build a team." That is the same role of a professional coach.

The benefits of coaching include gaining fresh perspectives on personal challenges, better decision-making skills, greater interpersonal effectiveness, and increased confidence. And, the list does not end there. Those who undertake coaching can expect better productivity, increased satisfaction with life and work, and the attainment of relevant goals. Like any professional athlete, every person with big goals should have a coach. For example, when writing this book, I worked with a writing coach. As a professional coach, speaker, consultant, strategist, and pastor, I work with an executive coach.

Importantly, coaching is not therapy or counseling. Coaching is future focused. While positive feelings/emotions may be a natural outcome of coaching, the primary focus is on creating actionable strategies for achieving specific goals in one's work or personal life. The emphases in a coaching relationship are on action, accountability, and follow through. With coaching, the assumption is that individuals or teams are capable of generating their own solutions, while the coach supplies supportive questions, approaches and resources.

Myth: I can't afford a coach.

Truth: Having a coach is an investment in myself. I can't afford not to have a coach.

Coaching Practice:

How could a coach help you? Take the next fifteen minutes to answer these questions.

1. In what areas of your life would you like to raise the bar?

_____
_____
_____
_____

2. What are the areas of your life where you have been saying, "I can't take this any more"?

_____

_____

_____

_____

3. What is an area in your life where you say, "I love this and want a lot more of this?"

_____

_____

_____

_____

4. What's the next BIG thing for you?

_____

_____

_____

_____

Who could potentially be your coach? (List at least two names.) When will you contact them to begin the process of engaging a coach?

_____

_____

_____

_____

_____

_____

_____

_____

_____

_____

20. Teach What You're Learning

I remember as a little girl playing the game "school" with my cousins. I loved being the teacher because it gave me a sense of being in charge and being knowledgeable. Although my cousins rarely sat quietly and listened to me speak I still loved pointing at the chalkboard and instructing. Afterwards, I would dismiss my cousins for recess. It was so much fun until someone else wanted to be the teacher. It was more fun for me to be the teacher than the student. Yet, I realized later in life, that the best teachers, first listen, and then speak. They are committed learners before becoming professors. I learned how to teach from watching teachers, coaches, and mentors in my life. I believe there's a bit of a teacher in all of us. We all have experiences and knowledge that can help others.

Teaching, mentoring or coaching is the essence of leadership. A leader is one who points others in a particular direction. My husband Kevin is a football coach. He teaches boys how to play football, but also how to listen and follow directions. He teaches them discipline and commitment. They learn goal setting and how to win and lose. Every August, I'm excited to see the group of boys gather together to be discipled in football and life. It is a great joy to see the fruit of his teaching when games are won and the boys and families get to celebrate. Of course, there are also times when games are lost and there are many life lessons in those experiences as well.

There is an impulse in each one of us to learn, teach and know our life is meaningful. We want to know we are worthy, loved and creative. Ultimately, all of these are spiritual desires only affirmed through relationships with God and one another. Thus, we all need a teacher, coach or mentor and we are all called to be teachers, coaches and mentors.

Many people don't know I am an introvert. To be an introvert means I get my energy from being alone, processing concepts and figuring things out in my head before interacting with others. It's not that I don't enjoy people. I actually love people, but it takes a great deal of energy and focus for me to be with others. It requires ample downtime. As an introvert, I love to grab a good book and sneak away to a quiet place to escape. I also enjoy activities I can do on my own like going for a run and watching the sunrise or finding a quiet coffee shop and enjoying a cappuccino. Yet, I've learned as much as I enjoy being alone, there is a richness of life I can only find when I engage with people. We are created to pursue God-sized dreams that can only be accomplished with the help of God and engaging with others.

We ponder questions such as, how can we make our communities richer in love? How can I make my community better? Who needs our help most? This is about giving our life away. I will be the first to admit this isn't always easy to figure out.

You're not a leader or teacher, you say? Your life experiences, good or bad, hold no value? Can anyone benefit from the mistakes you've made? These are questions we all struggle with. The shame of our mistakes or the fear of being judged for our mishaps hinders us from sharing our stories with others. Yet, by encouraging, teaching, and sharing, we help others and gain strength for our journey. This is the beginning of leaving a legacy.

Myth: I'm not a teacher. My life's story isn't worth telling.

Truth: Encouraging, teaching, and sharing with others, makes me stronger.

Coaching Practice:

There are people waiting to hear your story so they can learn and grow through you. Yet, sometimes people confuse the call to teach with the profession of teaching. Actually, no matter what your job or hobby, talents or gifts are, we are all called to be teachers using our own life stories.

Take time now and answer the following questions. What experiences have impacted your life most? Who needs to hear your story? What could they learn from you? Who could you imagine teaching? When will you start?

_____

_____

_____

_____

_____

Have the courage to start teaching today.

Part III: Eliminate:

How to discern and cut out limiting beliefs and actions that block a RISEN life?

As I write today I'm thinking of our daughter Alexis and how much she's grown up. At the young age of four, she is able to comprehend much of what's happening in life, especially with her brothers who she follows intently. Alexis has matured from an infant into a beautiful, smart, curious, and strong willed girl. She often reminds me that she's not a baby anymore. Alexis' maturing reminds me that growing in God's grace is a natural process. It's embedded in our DNA and happens every day even if we can't see it. Yet, I'm also remembering that to mature requires times of being uncomfortable. Alexis has endured restless nights, potty training, temper tantrums, and much more. Likewise, as women becoming the authors of our own lives, we will inevitably go through tears, trials, temptations, and tensions. There is no maturing without going through life's circumstances. And often, the tougher the trial the more we learn from the experience. One key to maturing is realizing our thoughts and beliefs create our reality. When our beliefs are empowering, we become powerful. When our beliefs are limiting, we experience fear, restriction and perceived failure in our lives. In this third section, we'll explore the most common limiting beliefs many women experience and then replace them with a truth. Notice the first step is identifying and acknowledging a limiting belief exists, not ignoring it. Importantly, our goal is not to overpower the limiting belief with willpower, but to release and replace the limiting belief with a new empowering belief.

Limiting beliefs are usually subconscious. They operate below the level of awareness. You'll typically notice them by their side effects. For example, when you've set ambitious goals and try to pursue them, and then hit barriers that slow or stop your progress. We also notice the side effects of limiting beliefs when we experience power struggles in our closest relationships with children, spouses, parents, and friends.

These deeply entrenched limiting beliefs must be released to become the author of your own life as a warrior chick. Remember, she is one who is her own unique expression of God's grace. She finds her wings and flies. Embracing, living and sharing empowering truths will free us to pursue what really matters. They will enable us to live at our highest level of purpose, vision and joy. Below are ten limiting beliefs that when removed, will transform your life.

Importantly, eliminating limiting beliefs and replacing them with truth is a deeply spiritual practice. It's not about a particular religion, theology, or doctrine. However, spiritual power, experienced in diverse ways, gives people the ability to recognize and celebrate truth, to be authentic, to love and to be loved. I recently ran across this quote on Pinterest and in Brene Brown's book, Rising Strong. I think it sums this point perfectly. "Grace will take you places hustling can't."

Read each section, complete the coaching exercises, and begin to practice your new beliefs. Ready. Set. Go.

21. I am not enough.
22. I am a failure.
23. Mistakes are bad.
24. Never let them see you sweat
25. I can't be happy until _____
26. What if they say no? I will be rejected.
27. I can't tell my truth.
28. I'm not strong enough.
29. I don't have a choice.
30. I can't forgive myself.

21. I am not enough.

One of the most significant experiences of my life has been pregnancy and childbirth. After a four-year journey with infertility, I remember the moment I found out I was pregnant with each of our three children. I also recall the agony of trying to get pregnant and not understanding why it wasn't happening. In those moments, I questioned my faith and myself. Some of the thoughts that ran through my mind were, "Maybe, I'm not woman enough or faithful enough." Kevin and I both desired to be parents and this desire was not just biological, it was spiritual. I believe we are created with a piece of God inside of us that gives us the desire to multiply. It is a desire to nurture, see things grow, and to leave a legacy. Yet, in this time of distress, many beliefs about myself were shaken at their core. I wondered if my life could be meaningful without being a mother.

Have you ever felt that you weren't _____ enough? Circle all that apply below:

Good enough

Smart enough

Powerful enough

Woman enough

Faithful enough

Loved enough

These are some of the most common limiting beliefs about being "enough" that women face. At the core of these limiting beliefs is fear. These fears often operate at a subconscious level like a thick fog that keeps hanging around. Some of the most common emotional fears we face include the following:

Check all that apply for you.

_____ Fear of failure and being seen as incompetent

_____ Fear of being ordinary

_____ Fear of being alone

_____ Fear of disappointing others

_____ Fear of rejection or abandonment

_____ Fear of losing control

_____ Fear of loss of privacy and being "exposed"

_____ Fear of too much responsibility

_____ Fear of scarcity and not having enough _____

_____ Fear of success

_____ Fear of death

So are you ready for the fog of fear and limiting beliefs to lift? Here are three steps towards your freedom.

1) Identify what fears exist below the surface for you.

One of the best ways to identify your fear is to answer the questions, "What am I not believing God for? Or where am I doubting myself?" These are clues to your deepest fears. In my case of infertility, I doubted if others would accept me as a woman if I didn't birth children. I doubted if Kevin would love me the same as his wife, if we didn't have children. I doubted if I could be at peace with myself without achieving the dream of motherhood that I held. What are you doubting?

_____

_____

_____

_____

2) Take quiet time to reflect.

As I've coached leaders and asked these questions, the answer I get most often when I ask about fears is, "I don't know." We're often so busy that we don't take time to examine our thoughts, feelings, and fears. We just keep plowing ahead instead of slowing down and being aware of the assumptions behind our actions. Yet, the path to consciousness requires taking time to examine both doing and being, action and the meaning behind the action.

Centered by Blue Cross and Blue Shield of Illinois is my favorite mobile applications (or apps) for breathing and meditation. It provides audio guided or self-guided meditation sessions and daily goals. Two of my favorite activities are the five-minute mindful walk and four-minute mini meditation. These quick exercises remind me to breathe, relax and retreat into a peaceful presence in the middle of busy days. It's a non-judgmental space for simply being. There is nothing to do, no decisions to make, and no one's requests to respond to. Meditation also helps train the brain to focus attention instead of multitasking. I've found after a few minutes of meditation, I am better able to see with clarity what's happening within myself. I realize my thoughts and emotions have power only by the meaning I give them (beliefs). This is the true beginning of transformation because beliefs lead to actions.

3) Replace fear with truth.

Here's the truth. YOU ARE ENOUGH, just as you are. We are created to be creators. In fact, we are co-creators with God. God blesses all of creation, which naturally grows and dies, creates again, and multiplies to extend itself through all of humanity and creation. We are good enough, smart enough, powerful enough, woman enough, faithful enough, and loved enough to be and do amazing things in this world. Will you believe it? What's your truth? See the truths below for each day of the week. Journal your thoughts below and recite the truths each day.

_____
_____
_____

Monday: I am authentic, dependable, capable and knowledgeable just as I am.

Tuesday: I am extraordinary.

Wednesday: I am never alone. I am accepted and loved.

Thursday: I am the author of my life.

Friday: I have what I need. I lack nothing.

Saturday: I welcome success.

Sunday: I cherish life and the divine within me.

22.   I'm a failure.

When we see famous people we often hear about their great success. We are enamored with money, cars, clothes, houses, and awards. Yet, we rarely acknowledge what it took to be successful. Michael Jordan, Thomas Edison, Oprah Winfrey, Abraham Lincoln, Steve Jobs and Eminem all experienced great failures in their life before they achieved success. Not once, but many times. At critical points in their journey, each one of them had to make a decision of failure or faith. Check out this YouTube video titled "Famous Failures."

http://www.youtube.com/watch?v=zLYECIjmnQs (2:58)

What story are you telling yourself? Are you a failure or faithful? Will stories of loss or learning dictate your future? Maybe you haven't yet become who you want to be or have as much money as you thought you'd have. Maybe your relationships haven't developed the way you'd like. Yet, will you be defined by failure or faith?

One of my favorite biblical stories is from Luke 18:1-8 where we encounter a woman who knows about failure. She is a widow. Throughout the bible, we encounter widows weeping (Job 27:15, Psalm 78:64), mourning (2 Samuel 14:2), in misery (Lamentations 1:1), in poverty (Ruth 1:21, 1 Kings 17:7-12, Job 22:9) and in debt (2 Kings 4:1) after the main source of her economic support, her husband, dies. Widows in the bible are frequently placed alongside the orphan and the immigrant (Exodus 22:21-22, Deuteronomy 24:17-21) as a representative of the poorest of the poor in the culture's social structure. Many widows felt hopeless and wore a robe and head covering as a sign of their destitute status (Genesis 38:14-19, 2 Sam 14:2). Check out bible.org for more insights on widows in the bible.

The widow in each of us is also real. Individually, and as a people, we know what it's like to be abandoned, economically distressed, depressed, and outcast. And yet, just like the widow, we have a choice to make. Will we allow what society deemed as a failure dictate our future or will we choose faith?

Myth: I've failed.

Truth: My best is yet to come.

As we eliminate the limiting belief of failure and replace it with faith, practice these two actions this week.

1) Look Ahead—Look ahead towards the blessing that is to come. The widow in Luke 18 had a sense that her story was not over. Even when society gave up on her, she did not give up on herself. We know this because she kept coming to the judge saying, "Grant me justice against my adversary" (Luke 18:3). This widow boldly spoke her truth. She audaciously appealed to the judge to intervene on her behalf. With persistence, she insisted the judge settle a matter between her and an enemy. We don't know what their dispute was about but we do know this widow was relentless in her attempts for someone to hear and do something for her. She risked public shame and humiliation to change her situation.

Jesus also looked ahead in faith instead of failure. He was able to endure the shame of being insulted, beaten, and hung on a cross because he knew it was NOT the end of the story. He knew new life was waiting for him on the other side of the cross. When we are hard-pressed on every side we must be able to look ahead and declare, "And we know that in all things God works for the good of those who love him, who have been called according to his purpose" (Romans 8:28). This will help you persevere just as the widow and Jesus did.

What do you see as you look ahead in your life?

_____

_____

_____

_____

_____

2) Pray Ahead - Jesus prefaces the story in Luke 18 by saying it is a "parable about their need to pray always and not to lose heart." When most people think of prayer, they think of asking God for something or begging for a miracle. Yet, to pray ahead is connecting with the spirit of God within and speaking positive beliefs about the desired outcome. Affirmative prayer is the same method of prayer Jesus taught when he said, "So I tell you, whatever you ask for in prayer, believe that you have received it, and it will be yours" (Mark 11:24). If, for example, one was to pray traditionally, one might say, "Please, God, help me find a job." In contrast, an affirmative prayer might be: "God, I thank you that I am guided to my right and perfect employment." Affirmative prayer reflects the certainty that we are each being led by God, despite any temporary appearances.

Metaphysicians believe thoughts transmit magnetic energy and this energy attracts other energy of the same frequency. Whether we are conscious of it or not, our thoughts are transmitting energy that is attracting more of the same. When we remain focused on what we DON'T have, we attract more of the same. Yet, praying ahead will draw those things God desires for us into our life. We put power and intensity into our thought, and believe in the guidance we are receiving. Rosemary Ellen Guiley, author of Prayer Works, states that affirmative prayer "sets into motion the forces that enable us to manifest what we pray for. We pray to align ourselves with God and to allow ourselves to be inwardly guided to that good. Through affirmative prayer, we help co-create the good that is possible in our lives."

What's your prayer as yourself in this season?

_____

_____

_____

_____

_____

3) Act Ahead - I love that this "helpless" woman would not be stilled. She did not sit in her room paralyzed with tears and sorrow. She would not let the arrogant judge get away with being heartless. She would not be discouraged. Her hope was not fleeting, but rigorous. If an unjust judge granted vindication because someone hounded him, how much more God can bless us with? The question is, will you allow fear or faith to be your affirmation? We persist in justice, not only for ourselves, also for the weak, the outcast, the lonely, the distressed. Will our faith allow us to not give up even when it's not about us? Failure or faith, which will you choose? What are your next steps?

_____

_____

_____

_____

_____

Here's what I know for sure. Nothing worthwhile or significant enough to impact time and eternity will ever come to pass without persevering in faith. This is the message we get from the life of Jesus who persevered. It is a persevering faith that empowers us to fulfill God's will for our life, our church, our community. That's success. Your best is yet to come.

23.   Mistakes are bad.

It was November 28, 2008. We had just celebrated Thanksgiving the day before with family. We enjoyed food, laughter, and anticipated the arrival of Aaron, our second son. At nine months, I was very pregnant. Aaron's due date was one week away. However, around 11 p.m., the waters trickled as a sharp pain in my abdomen intensified. I clinched the armrest as Kevin drove us to the hospital, my fingernails sunk into the leather seats. I groaned and moaned as another contraction came. Finally, the top of the hospital shone and all I could say was, "Jesus!" The waters continued to trickle as the pain, sharp as a nail, pierced my side and would not subside. "Jesus!" The pain felt like death was near, but it was life that was actually about to appear. At 1 a.m., Aaron was born.

After Aaron's birth, I reflected back on the moment I found out I was pregnant with him. I was not sure if the time was right. Isaac was only two years old and our life had been chaotic with jobs, travel, and parenting. We were just starting to feel a sense of peace after what seemed like a roller coaster ride. I secretly wondered if it was a mistake to have another child. Have you ever wondered if you were making a huge mistake? Even the anguish of fearing a bad decision is enough to make me feel sick. Though often, through what may seem like a mistake, new life is about to appear.

In Luke 23:34, Jesus was near death. His withered body torn, cut, and slowly bleeding to death would never be the same. The waters of his body trickled out. The pain intensified as nails pierced his side, he gasped for breath, and said, "Father forgive them for they know not what they do."

Maybe you've read this familiar text before, Jesus praying to God as he did on many occasions. In fact, Jesus taught his disciples how to pray on a mountain. Jesus showed his disciples how to pray in a garden; and Jesus is now giving himself in prayer on a cross. Praying is nothing new for Jesus. This may seem ordinary, until we put ourselves on the cross with Jesus. It is on the cross we discover how shocking this prayer really is.

Who was Jesus talking about when he said, "Forgive THEM?" Who is them? Is it the Jewish religious leaders? The Roman political power players? The soldiers who carried out the dirty work? The people who shouted, "Crucify him?" The disciples who deserted him? Or could it be...you and me?

What did Jesus mean when he said, "FORGIVE them?" Did Jesus, as he hung dying on a tree, mean that the lies they told should be overlooked? That the prejudiced trial he received should be forgotten? That the soldiers who whipped, stripped and hung him should be surrendered from any responsibility? That the people who shouted, "Crucify him" should still be friends? That the sins of the liar, thief, and murderer should be canceled?

It is not just that Jesus said forgive them. He said, "They know NOT what they do." How can they not know that they arrested him, denied him, mocked him, beat him, lied on him, and hung him on a tree to die? How can THEY not know what they do? How could WE not know what WE do?

It is often challenging for us as humans to forgive. We are not God. We are much better at wallowing in judgment of our own mistakes. We want revenge when others hurt us. So how do we forgive our own and others' thoughts, words, and actions that we perceive as mistakes?

One answer comes from a word in South Africa, "Ubuntu." Ubuntu describes the essence of being human. It is an African philosophy of community, interconnectedness, mutual respect, solidarity and caring of humanity and serves as the spiritual foundation of many African societies. South African professor Dirk J. Louw writes, "It both describes human being as 'being-with-others' and prescribes what 'being-with-others' should be all about." In other words, being fully human is only possible when we are in relationship with a community of people, both believers and non-believers in Christ. Louw emphasizes the context of Ubuntu in African culture is both secular and religious and is a model of life and a way of looking at the world. One of the traditions of Ubuntu is when someone does something wrong, they take the person to the center of the village. There the tribe surrounds the individual for two days, while members of the tribe speak all of the good that the person has done in their lifetime. The tribe believes each person is good, yet sometimes people make mistakes, which are actually cries for help. They join in this ritual to encourage the person to reconnect with their true nature. The belief is that unity and affirmation are more powerful to change behavior than shaming or punishment.

How can we apply Ubuntu in our daily lives?

First, we must reimagine what we label as mistakes. Just like in my pregnancy with Aaron, we all have thoughts of doubt. Yet, in time, we realize every experience is an opportunity for growth and healing, not a mistake. Our family has been richly blessed by Aaron's presence. He is the most amazing and creative son we could have ever dreamed of. I can't imagine our life without him. I have been transformed through the privilege of loving Aaron.

Myth: Mistakes are bad.

Truth: My "mistakes" are actually blessings that lead to new life.

Take the next fifteen minutes to answer to these questions.

Describe a mistake in your life. What happened? How did it feel at the time?

_____

_____

_____

_____

_____

Looking back now, how has that situation been a blessing? How has it shaped your life?

_____

_____

_____

_____

24.   I can never let them see me sweat.

As I write today, it's basketball season and Isaac and Aaron are practicing or playing games almost every night. They both play on competitive teams and spend hours in gyms each week. They are often competing against athletes who are older, taller and just as determined as they are to win. We've experienced the thrill of victory and the agony of defeat. We've seen both boys make amazing plays at the end of the game and secure a win. We've also seen them take the last shot and miss. That's heartbreaking. After those heartbreaks, both boys wonder if their team still believes in them. They also quietly wonder if Kevin and I, as parents, are mad at them and still love them. That may sound extreme to us as adults, but any kid that's competed in sports has wondered if they'll be accepted or rejected if they lose. As adults, we have the same fear of rejection and need for acceptance, especially when we lose.

Earvin "Magic" Johnson, Jr., born August 14, 1959, is a retired point guard for the Los Angeles Lakers of the National Basketball Association (NBA). After winning championships in high school and college, he was selected first overall in the 1979 NBA Draft by the Lakers and played for thirteen seasons. He won five NBA championships with the Lakers during the 1980s and many other accolades. He was "Magic" and all over the world, people cheered, "Magic, Magic, Magic!" On Thursday, Nov. 7, 1991, the cheering stopped for Magic Johnson when he announced he was HIV-positive and would be retiring from basketball immediately. There was no hosanna. Magic could not save himself or anyone else.

Magic said telling his wife Cookie he was HIV-positive was the most difficult thing in his life, "I played against the best in basketball: Michael Jordan, Larry Bird... shoot, I thought that was going to be the most difficult thing to do. Those things were nothing. The most difficult thing in my life was driving from the doctor's office to tell my wife Cookie, I had HIV." The cheering from his wife stopped in that moment.

Magic said this about the reaction of some friends, "I would call people, 'Let's work out.' They always had something to do. 'Oh no, I can't right now because I've got to get ready for the game or whatever.' Can you imagine that? I played one-on-one my whole life and now I'm looking for someone to play one-on-one with." The cheering from his friends stopped in that moment.

What do you do in your life when the cheering stops from the people around you? What happens when you no longer have a "hosanna" in your soul? What happens in moments of defeat?

Myth: I can never let them see me sweat.

Truth: I am authentic and brave. Authenticity makes me strong.

To be authentic and brave requires risk. If we're going to engage in the game of life and play big, not small, we're going to experience heartache. If we're creative and try new paths, some will lead to dead ends. If we want to be extraordinary, we must be willing to take the last shot and sometimes miss. And, we can be honest about how that feels. A quote I recently saw on Pinterest by Mindy Hale sums this up well—"Let people see the real, imperfect, flawed, quirky, weird, beautiful, magical person that you are." We must not be afraid to let others see us struggle and persevere. When we let other people see the real us, we give them permission to be their magical selves too. Our goal is progress and authenticity not perfection. This builds trust and this is our power.

How will you practice authenticity? Take fifteen minutes now to journal and answer the following questions.

When have you recently thought that you couldn't be your authentic self and "let them see you sweat"? How did this feel? How can this situation make you stronger and more resilient?

_____
_____
_____
_____
_____
_____
_____
_____
_____
_____
_____
_____
_____
_____
_____
_____

25.   I can't be happy until _____.

It's January and I'm reflecting on the holidays that recently passed. I enjoyed spending lots of time at home during Thanksgiving, Christmas, and New Years. We visited my hometown in St. Louis for Christmas for the first time in many years. To be with family, felt like a warm fluffy blanket wrapped around my shoulders on a cold snowy night. We all yearn to feel at "home." Home is a place full of love, security, comfort, and rest. Sometimes "home" is found in a place like a familiar city. More often, "home" is about being with people who make us feel loved, secure, and comforted. It is a place of rest. During seasons where we experience loss and sadness, "home" may seem impossible to find and feelings of unsettledness set in. We quietly wonder if we will ever be happy in our current situation. We wonder if we're being punished. We feel exiled from home.

In one of my favorite scriptures in Jeremiah chapter 29 verses 1-14, we meet a group of people who are yearning for "home" after being banished from their homes, family, and friends and taken against their will to a foreign country as refugees living in poverty. The people expected the exile to last only a short time, at most, the length of one generation. Yet, the exile lasted much longer and the Israelites were filled with grief and anxiety.

So what do we do in the midst of our own exiles when feelings of "home" are nowhere to be found?

Myth: I can't be happy until my relationship, job, finances, or health gets better.

Truth: Home (love, security, and comfort) is available right where I am.

Here's a way to cultivate joy wherever you are today.

Surrender your current situation to God. God tells the exiles they should settle and make new homes, even if they are temporary, in their place of exile. Here are God's instructions: Build houses and live in them; plant gardens and eat what you grow; settle down, get married, have families. Don't let your numbers decline. In short, don't stop living. Don't wait until an elusive "some day" to get on with the business of continuing to be God's covenant people.

Maybe the most challenging command of all: "But seek the welfare of the city where I have sent you into exile, and pray to the Lord on its behalf, for in its welfare you will find your welfare" (29:7). HOME IS WHERE WE MAKE IT. We do not have to wait until we get the perfect house, perfect job, perfect relationship, perfect health nor perfect bank account to be home. Jeremiah reminded the people that it was not a betrayal of God or yourself to create "home" right where you are, even if it's not your ideal place. Home is where you make it.

Jeremiah stated the exile would last seventy years or three and a half generations. This meant when Jerusalem was finally rebuilt and they returned home, it would be the great-grandchildren of the original exiles, along with their children, who returned.

Jeremiah also reminded the people they were not exiled from God. In Babylon, they could see the temples of other gods. He encouraged them to accept their role in a foreign land while maintaining the faith practices of Israel. Jeremiah said when they call, pray, search, and seek. God will respond by restoring them to their home. This was not just a physical place. Home is an internal place of the soul where we no longer feel like an outsider because we are loved by God. It is a place of safety because we are not alone. Wherever you are today, find new rest and make it home.

How can you surrender your current situation to God?

_____

_____

_____

_____

_____

_____

_____

_____

Pray: God of hope, sometimes I feel like I'm in exile, separated from the joy of your presence. Restore me and let me find you when I seek you. Create home within me filled with sweet peace now and forever. Amen.

_____

_____

_____

_____

_____

_____

_____

_____

26. What if they say, no? I will be rejected.

As a little girl, I learned about the tradition of call and response through music in church. Let me give you an example. Sing with me right where you are. I'll sing a line and then you sing the next one. Let's repeat it three times.

Call: This little light of mine.

Response: I'm gonna let it shine.

Call: This little light of mine.

Response: I'm gonna let it shine.

Call: This little light of mine.

Response: I'm gonna let it shine.

All: Let it shine. Let is shine. Let it shine.

Call and response is a form of "spontaneous verbal and non-verbal interaction between speaker and listener in which the "calls" are followed by "responses" from the people listening. Let's try it again.

In this most famous call and response chant type song, the "preacher" in church sings the first line and the "congregation" echoes with a response.

Call: Swing low, sweet chariot

Response: Coming for to carry me home

Call: Swing low, sweet chariot

Response: Coming for to carry me home

In African and African American cultures, call-and-response is a pervasive pattern not just in music, but also in public gatherings, in the discussion of civic affairs, in religious rituals, as well as in gospel, blues, rhythm and blues, jazz, and hip-hop music. During slavery, people's very survival was dependent upon call and response. Through call and response, slaves coordinated their labor, communicated with one another across adjacent fields, lifted exhausted spirits, and expressed the joy and hope, pain and sorrow of their condition.

What does call and response have to do with the fear of rejection? Often we fail to "call" forth the best in ourselves because we are fearful of not getting the response we want from others. We don't say, "I love you" because we fear the other person won't return the love. We don't apply for a new job because we fear the response will be, "no." We don't speak up when we see injustice because we fear being an outcast.

Myth: If they say no, I am rejected.

Truth: I am accepted just as I am. I am free to be authentically ME no matter what the response.

As we become the author of our own lives we must embrace that my "call" doesn't depend on someone else's "response." Being authentic is all that's required. Two quotes I recently saw on Pinterest sums up this value well:

"Rejection doesn't mean you aren't good enough; it means the other person failed to notice what you have to offer."

"Some people are going to reject you, simply because you shine too bright for them. And that's okay. Keep shining."

So how will you practice self-acceptance? Take fifteen minutes now to journal and answer the following questions.

What has the fear of how others may respond prevented you from doing? What action can you take now to move towards your dreams?

_____

_____

_____

_____

_____

_____

_____

_____

_____

_____

_____

_____

_____

_____

_____

_____

_____

_____

_____

_____

_____

27.   I can't tell my truth.

There's a story from Ethiopia about a boy named Miobe (which means the Frightened One). He is sad because he thinks he is a coward. So Miobe decides to take a journey to find courage. Along the journey, he faces challenges and with each challenge, he gains greater self-confidence. His last challenge is a monster that lives in a cave at the top of a mountain. Everyone in the village below is scared of the monster and paralyzed with fear, but Miobe offers to kill the monster for them. When he first sees the monster, it is the size of three huge dinosaurs and smoke is curling from its nostrils. Frightened, Miobe keeps climbing but decides not to look at the monster until he is halfway up the mountain; else, he might be too scared to approach the beast.

When he looks next, the monster is only the size of one dinosaur (which is still pretty big). The monster snorts flame at him, Miobe panics and is halfway to the foot of the mountain before he can make his feet stop running. When he looks again, the monster is the size of five huge dinosaurs.

Miobe finds it curious that the monster grows smaller when he approaches and bigger when he runs away. He thinks perhaps, if he gets close enough, the monster might grow small enough for him to kill it with his dagger. To keep from being too scared, the boy closes his eyes tight and runs up the hill, fast before he can change his mind. When he opens his eyes, he is at the opening of the cave, but sees no monster. He enters the cave and sees nothing to be afraid of. He wonders if he ran to the wrong cave when he feels something hot touch his foot. He looks down and sees the monster, now the size of a baby kitten. He picks it up and it curls up in his palm, making a gentle sound halfway between a purr and a bubbling kettle. The boy decides to keep it for a pet. With the monster asleep in his hands, he returns to the village. The people hail him as a monster slayer, but he says he didn't need to slay it. Awestruck, they gather to look at the creature. He explains how it grew larger when he ran away and smaller when he approached. A young girl asks, "What's its name?" Miobe didn't think to ask. The monster wakes, yawning a puff of smoke, looks around at the people and says in a voice as clear as a bell, "Some people call me worry, some call me anxiety, and some call me doubt. But most people call me fear."

Source: Unknown

One of our greatest fears in life is being judged by others and then rejected. I faced this fear when I left a lucrative career in marketing to pursue a vocation of coaching leaders and ministry. One day, early in this transition, I wrote this in my journal.

"Here I am, Lord, alone with you. This is a barren and lonely place sometimes. At other times it is a warm and reassuring place. I'm at a point in my life that I surrender all that I am. I have no rights. I am nobody. God, you are my everything. Hold me, guide me, teach me to be who you're calling me to be. I am an empty vessel. Into your hands I commit my spirit."

I remember this time vividly. I felt alone and doubted if I could tell my truth. I assumed most would not understand. I sought refuge in solitude and experienced moments of strength and some of fear, just like Miobe.

Through journaling, worship, prayer, fasting, and study, I discerned my truth and gained courage to share it boldly. This was the beginning of becoming the author of my own life. Here's the declaration I wrote in worship and prayer just a few days after the previous writing.

"My Spirit shakes! God I am full of you! I feel a new boldness, a new urging to do your will, to preach your Word! To do your dance like David! I will worship and praise you with all that I am! I am sold out to your will! Yes, Lord, I am free! Nothing holds me! I pray with authority and power from You! I speak healing and see bodies and spirits being healed. I speak life into children and watch them grow! Oh God! Freedom is available to me and everyone I touch through You. Not by my power or my might, but you who are all powerful! You are my ONE thing!"

Myth: I can't tell my truth.

Truth: My truth sets me free.

Take fifteen minutes now to journal and answer the following questions.

So what's your truth? How is God calling you forth from fear to faith? What monster must be slayed for you to be free?

_____

_____

_____

_____

_____

28. I'm not strong enough.

As a sixteen-year-old girl in the summer of 1989, I remember the agony and embarrassment of collapsing during a two-mile track race. I had run this race many times since I was eight years old. For whatever reason, on this day my body shut down during the last stretch of the eight-lap race. I down shifted from running to walking to barely being able to stand. Finally, my dad and brother ran onto the track and carried me off. I had never experienced a day like this. I was a strong distance runner. How could I now be so weak?

My experience running reminds me of a story titled Potatoes, Eggs & Coffee. Once upon a time, a daughter complained to her father that her life was miserable and that she didn't know how she was going to make it. She was tired of fighting and struggling all the time. It seemed just as one problem was solved, another one soon followed.

Her father, a chef, took her to the kitchen. He filled three pots with water and placed each on a high fire. Once the three pots began to boil, he placed potatoes in one pot, eggs in the second pot, and ground coffee beans in the third pot. He then let them sit and boil, without saying a word to his daughter.

The daughter moaned and impatiently waited, wondering what her father was doing. After twenty minutes, he turned off the burners, took the potatoes out of the pot and placed them in a bowl. He pulled the eggs out and placed them in a bowl and then ladled the coffee into a cup.

Turning to his daughter he asked, "Daughter, what do you see?"

"Potatoes, eggs, and coffee," she hastily replied.

"Look closer," he said, "and touch the potatoes." She did, noting the potatoes were soft.

He then asked her to take an egg and break it. After pulling off the shell, she observed the hard-boiled egg.

Finally, he asked her to sip the coffee. Its rich aroma brought a smile to her face.

"Father, what does this mean?" she asked.

Her father explained that the potatoes, the eggs, and coffee beans had each faced the same adversity, the boiling water. However, each one reacted differently.

The potato went in strong, hard and unrelenting, but in boiling water it became soft and weak. The egg was fragile with the thin outer shell protecting its liquid interior until it was put in the boiling water. There, the inside of the egg became hard.

However, the ground coffee beans were unique. After they were exposed to the boiling water, they changed the water and created something new.

"Which are you?" he asked his daughter. "When adversity knocks on your door, how do you respond? Are you a potato, an egg, or a coffee bean?"

We all face challenges in our lives, illnesses, job losses, and grief from the loss of loved ones that are all too real. These times can either make us weaker, bitter, or stronger. These times reveal our deepest limiting thoughts about ourselves.

Myth: I am not strong enough.

Truth: I am stronger than my struggle. Struggles cultivate strength.

In my running life, after a time of rest, I returned to training. The doctor diagnosed me with dehydration and advised me to drink adequate water and ease back into running. That fall, I returned to school and training with the cross-country team. I decided, with the strength of God, to be created new like the coffee bean. I became more conscious of my body, resilient in my soul, and grateful for the gift of running.

This spiritual truth reminds me of the scripture in John 15:4-5, "Abide in me as I abide in you. Just as the branch cannot bear fruit by itself unless it abides in the vine, neither can you unless you abide in me. I am the vine, you are the branches. Those who abide in me and I in them bear much fruit, because apart from me you can do nothing." Through faith, adversity makes us stronger.

Take fifteen minutes now to journal and answer the following questions.

Write about a time adversity knocked you down. Did you respond like a potato, an egg, or a coffee bean? What did you learn about yourself from this experience?

_____

_____

29. I don't have a choice.

Most mornings I wake up, drag myself out of bed, brush my teeth, change into my exercise clothes, have a drink of water and make my way towards the treadmill. I do this with very little thinking. Next, I shower, wake up the kids, get everyone dressed, grab a quick breakfast and we're out the door for school and work. I work for eight to ten hours, take kiddos to practices, make or grab dinner, get homework done, shower and finally collapse in bed about 11 pm. And, I forgot to mention the hundreds of times I check my text, email, Facebook, Instagram, and Twitter accounts each day. These are routine daily choices that I don't think much about. I just do what needs to be done. I feel a deep responsibility to myself, family, colleagues, and community to do these things and I sometimes feel guilty when I can't do them all perfectly. Subconsciously, I often tell myself I don't have a choice, this is just life. Like me, you also make hundreds of small and big decisions everyday. You decide whether or not to get out of bed, exercise, eat, what to think about and what to do. We often make these decisions in an effort to keep everyone happy, whether we admit it or not. And, it's easier to relinquish responsibility for our lives than to grapple with real trade-offs and make tough decisions.

In my work as an executive coach, I have coached many "successful" leaders who are consumed and overwhelmed by the pressures all around them. They are working frantically to do everything perfectly, now. Many began their work inspired and have since become snared by unrealistic personal and professional expectations. The "have to dos" consume most hours of their day and they feel helpless.

Myth: I don't have a choice. I have to do it all.

Truth: I am in control of my own choices. I enjoy my journey, not just the destination.

Being the author of our own lives means we deliberately choose our own life-giving path. This is a pathway to liberation and freedom. As Greg Mckeown in his book, Essentialism writes, "The way of the Essentialist means living by design, not by default. Instead of making choices reactively, the Essentialist deliberately distinguishes the vital few from the trivial many, eliminates the nonessentials, and then removes obstacles so the essential things have clear, smooth passage."

Spiritually, in Deuteronomy 30:19 (NIV), God says, "This day I call the heavens and the earth as witnesses against you that I have set before you life and death, blessings and curses. Now choose life, so that you and your children may live." Every choice has consequences that impact life and death of our mind, body, and soul. If we want to live a purposeful and fulfilling life, we must make our own thoughtful and wise choices. A quote I recently read on Pinterest captures this well — "Freedom isn't the ability to say, 'Yes'. It's the ability to say, 'No.'"

So how will you make new choices? Take fifteen minutes now to journal and answer the following questions.

What is most important in your life right now (not in the future)?

_____

_____

_____

_____

_____

How can you be more present in your life today?

_____

_____

_____

_____

_____

What can you eliminate now to make room for what's most important?

_____

_____

_____

_____

_____

_____

_____

_____

_____

_____

_____

_____

_____

_____

30.   I can't forgive myself.

It's a few weeks before Valentine's Day. The media has declared this is the season of love. Candy and dinner. Hugs and smiles. Gifts and cards. These are beautiful acts of love. Yet, sometimes the hardest being to love is ourselves. Sometimes our greatest enemy is within. The greatest struggles are not outside, but within. It's easier to love other people, money, cars, clothes, houses, and jobs than it is to truly be free and to love ourselves.

Some years ago, I ran across an article titled, "Self-Hate Patterns" on the website dailystrength.org. The images below from the article capture the struggle of love and forgiveness well. I've edited the original text for clarity.

The Doormat - The Doormat lets others walk over them. They may question their value in the world, or they place their value in how much they're getting walked on, and how well they can take it. In this way, she avoids the real feelings of unworthiness, because the person can tell themselves they have value because they're being selfless and generous and caring of other's feelings. What they're actually doing is negating their own needs and rights (and often boundaries and property) and allowing others to occupy the space they should keep for themselves by divine right. Sacrifices that are not appreciated and that end with rejection are primary with this pattern.

The Punching Bag - The Punching Bag accepts physical pain/punishment as inevitable. They anticipate the blows, and like an animal that has been beaten, goes into a submissive stance before a hand can even be raised. When the blows come, there's a sense of relief. Waiting and anticipating it creates horrible fear and tension.

The Garbage Can - The Garbage Can allows themselves to be "dumped on." Husbands, wives, bosses, even children are allowed to scoff, scorn, belittle, put down, make fun of, rage at and blame the Garbage Can for what goes wrong. People may excuse it because it's not physical. But it is still abuse, and the effects are JUST as harmful.

The Bad Girl/Boy - The Bad Girl/Boy plays the social outcast, the whore, the criminal, the Incorrigible One. Their energy makes them defiant in their "badness," and they often flaunt it in outrageous ways. They can even feel superior to the "good" people and make a big show of pretending they don't care about being accepted. But the truth is they do care, and deep down they believe they will never be accepted.

The Lonely One – The Lonely One is the social outcast, but unlike the Bad Girl/Boy, the Lonely Ones are often never seen. They are Alone. They feel (and sometimes are) invisible. They speak with soft voices that nobody really hears. They never seem to find love and even family relationships are outside their reach. They long for companionship and love and warmth and sharing. But they don't believe they deserve it or can ever find it. They walk alone, and they believe they will always be alone, forever.

The Great One - This is the pendulum swing into grandiosity in the person who is trying desperately to avoid how totally valueless they feel. They push their self-doubt away, stuff it into a corner of the attic, and walk through life in the better-than illusion. Everything is GREAT! They've overcome it all, have no problems, and in fact, are doing better than most other people. They may pretend they're not doing it, but a secret voice of judgment is running all the time. Often this pattern is so successful at creating the illusion of Big and Great and Wonderful and Oh-So-Powerful, that most in the person's life is fooled. The crash, when it comes, is usually heavy and deeply devastating.

The Critical Voice - This is often a constant running critical energy in the background. We may not hear it during the day when we are active and busy. It may only come to our awareness at quiet times, like when we're preparing for sleep, or trying to meditate. This is when self-hate brings forth all the things that it has been saving up, all the things we have ever done or said that we feel bad about. It may replay old scenes and conversations when you said something stupid or caused someone pain.

Myth: I can't forgive myself and I deserve punishment. I am guilty.

Truth: I am forgiven. I am whole. I am loved.

Embracing self-love and forgiveness is essential to becoming the author of your own life. So how will you begin to love yourself? Take fifteen minutes now to journal and answer the following questions.

Where do see you yourself in the images above? How does this make you feel?

_____

_____

_____

What new images will you embrace for yourself? Circle the ones that fit you or create your own.

Old Image	New Loving Image
Doormat	Door opener
Punching Bag	Precious Jewel
Garbage Can	Beautiful One
Lonely One	Fulfilled
Great One	Loved One
Bad Girl	Good Girl
Critical Voice	Affirming Voice

The poem below by Marianne Williamson in A Course in Miracles is one of my favorites. It's a tool to affirm our loveliness. Pray this remembering that when we forgive and love ourselves, we are healed. When we are healed, we can love others and be agents of their healing.

"Our deepest fear is not that we are inadequate. Our deepest fear is that we are powerful beyond measure. It is our light, not our darkness that most frightens us. We ask ourselves, Who am I to be brilliant, gorgeous, talented, fabulous? Actually, who are you not to be? You are a child of God. Your playing small does not serve the world. There is nothing enlightened about shrinking so that other people won't feel insecure around you. We are all meant to shine, as children do. We were born to make manifest the glory of God that is within us. It's not just in some of us; it's in everyone. And as we let our

118

own light shine, we unconsciously give other people permission to do the same. As we are liberated from our own fear, our presence automatically liberates others."

_____

_____

_____

_____

_____

_____

_____

_____

_____

_____

_____

_____

_____

_____

_____

_____

_____

_____

_____

_____

Part IV: Expand

How to practice and share the risen life?

Our fate is shaped from within ourselves outward, never from without inward.

- Jacques Lusseyran, French author and political activist

In this fourth section we'll explore ten exercises that will enable you to grow in your spiritual awareness, personal consciousness, and public ability to emerge as the author of your own life. Importantly, this journey begins internally and then manifests itself outwardly. Through these exercises you will discover new qualities about yourself and practice a life that you will find deeply rewarding. Remember after all the introspection you've done to take play breaks along the way. You've probably heard that play is essential for brain development in children. Playtime is also important to spur creativity and reduce stress in adults. So grab a friend. Play with Legos, Play Doh, or paint and see what you can create together just for the fun of it. Your mind, body and soul will thank you.

The 10 exercises are summarized below. Enjoy.

31.   Develop your Guiding Principles.
32.   Identify your passion.
33.   Find what inspires you.
34.   Claim your True Values.
35.   Call your mother.
36.   Create your mission statement.
37.   Create your book covers.
38.   Get balanced and focused.

39. Challenge yourself.
40. Create a keepsake.

31. Develop your Guiding Principles.

These are sometimes known as "ground rules." This is a personal covenant with yourself that will help you stay focused on your goals. Remember to be kind to yourself. The same grace you extend to yourself you will be able to share with others. Examples of guiding principles that I developed for myself are:

☐   I am patient with myself and choose to enjoy the journey.

☐   I make my personal and spiritual growth a priority each day.

☐   I slow down and hear the voice of God in nature.

☐   I have the courage to say "no" to things that do not align with my highest values.

☐   I keep my husband and children as first priority in my life.

☐   I have a coach to support me along my personal and professional journey.

☐   I live an extraordinary life.

In the space below, develop your list of Guiding Principles for your journey.

_____
_____
_____
_____
_____
_____
_____
_____

Lia McIntosh

32.   Identify your passion.

Passion is what inspires you. It is already within you, because it's <u>who</u> you are. This exercise is designed to unearth your passion that's beneath the surface using the photos on your phone or digital camera. Open the photo roll on your phone or camera. Select the last 50 photos you took that don't contain friends or family. Maybe it's a stunning sunrise you saw or a screen shot of a quote on a billboard. Then, take 50 note cards (3x5 or 4x6) and describe each photo using words or images. For example, draw the sunset and color it yellow or transcribe the quote. Use one index card to capture each photo. Next, look for patterns across all of your cards. Identify 2-5 themes and group the cards. In the space below, write your themes. These are clues to your life's passion.

_____

_____

_____

_____

_____

_____

_____

_____

_____

_____

_____

_____

_____

_____

_____

_____

33. Find what inspires you.

Inspiration comes from all around. Each of us have people whose presence inspires us to a higher calling. In this exercise you'll identify fifteen people who light you up (personal friends, public figures, or people you follow on Instagram/Facebook). Write the names or draw an image symbolizing each person and two words that describe the emotion you feel in their presence. Next, look for patterns across all of your cards. Identify 2-5 themes and group the cards. In the space below, write your themes. These are clues as to what inspires you.

_____

_____

_____

_____

_____

_____

_____

_____

_____

_____

_____

_____

_____

_____

_____

_____

_____

_____

34. Claim your True Values.

Values reflect <u>who</u> you really are. They are not who you'd like to become or you wish you were. Your values are the behaviors and activities you naturally express in good times or bad.

☐ Step 1: Read the list of values and circle 10 that resonate with you. You are looking for a "must" that's essential for you to be authentic. Ask yourself, "If I had this, would I be inspired?"

☐ Step 2: Narrow your values to 3. Which ones, when honored, take priority over the others? Highlight the 3 that are most important to you today.

Accountability	Dignity	Justice	Responsibility
Achievement	Diversity	Knowledge	Results
Adaptability	Empathy	Leadership	Reverence
Advancement	Energy	Learning	Risk Taking
Adventure	Enthusiasm	Listening	Safety
Attentiveness	Entrepreneurship	Long-term view	Security
Authority	Environmental Awareness	Love	Service
Balance	Ethics	Loyalty	Socializing
Being the Best	Fairness	Making a difference	Spirituality
Belonging	Faith	Money	Stamina
Caring	Family	Opportunities	Status
Caution	Friendship	Organization	Success
Challenge	Focus	Partnering	Teamwork
Collegiality	Forgiveness	Peace	Tolerance

Values List[1]

Collaboration	Honesty	Positivity	Tradition
Community	Humor/Fun	Power	Trust
Compassion	Improvement	Prestige	Unity
Competition	Independence	Productivity	Variety
Confidence	Influence	Profit	Vision
Contribution	Initiative	Purpose	Wealth
Control	Innovation	Quality	Winning
Cooperation	Integrity	Recognition	Wisdom
Creativity	Intelligence	Resilience	
Customer Satisfaction	Involvement	Respect	

Values List (cont'd)

Step 3: Define each value. Ask yourself, "Why is this value important to me?" Write down 3 specific reasons for each value. Next, ask "Who am I when I am this value?" Write down 3 specific reasons for each value.

_____

_____

_____

_____

_____

_____

_____

_____

_____

_____

Step 4: Honor your values. Set one goal for the next 12

_____

[1] *Source: Coach U resources, http://www.coachinc.com*

months that honors each of your top 3 values. The objective here is to only have value-based goals. If you have a goal that doesn't fit with one of your top 3 values, either adapt the goal to fit the value or let it go and come up with another goal.

_____

_____

_____

_____

_____

_____

_____

_____

_____

_____

_____

_____

_____

_____

_____

_____

_____

_____

_____

_____

_____

_____

35.   Call your mother.

Each person is created with unique talents, gifts, and experiences. There is no one like you. In this exercise you'll capture the characteristics about yourself that set you apart. As part of your discovery, call your mother (or someone who knows you from childhood) and ask, "What made me unique as a child?" Listen and take notes during the conversation. Use note cards (3x5 or 4x6) to write words that describe what your mom shared. Next, look for patterns across all of your cards. Identify 2-5 themes and group the cards. In the space below, write your themes. These are clues to your distinctiveness. Remember, you are beautiful, one of a kind, and handcrafted by God.

_____

_____

_____

_____

_____

_____

_____

_____

_____

_____

_____

_____

_____

_____

_____

_____

36. *Create your mission statement.*

In this exercise you'll take your guiding principles, passion, inspiration, values, and uniqueness and turn them into a personal mission statement. Your mission statement explains WHY you are doing what you do. Develop your statement using the following 3 steps:

☐ Step 1: Begin your statement with a VERB.
o "My mission is to _____."
☐ Step 2: Name three of your talents/gifts/abilities/expertise using NOUNS
o "I do this through _____."
☐ Step 3: Define WHO you want to make a contribution to in the world and HOW they will benefit.
o "So that, _____.

Example: *My mission is to inspire and equip people. I do this through coaching, speaking, writing, and teaching actionable systems for growth, so that leaders are confident, passionate, and able to make a lasting impact at work, home and in the world*

37.   *Create your book covers.*

Your book covers describe in one quick glance the vision of your life. In this exercise you'll stand on the balcony and take a 50,000-foot view of your life using all you've discovered thus far. Using the themes within your discovery, design 4 book covers that depict the vision for your life. It may include an image, word or colorful design that captures your heart. In the space below draw your book covers. Be as colorful, fun, and detailed as you like. These are clues to your distinctiveness (and possibly books you'll actually write one day).

38.   Get balanced and focused.

Balance is personal and unique to each individual. What may be satisfying or balanced for you may be stressful or boring for others. This exercise will help raise your awareness, clarify your priorities, and plan a life that is deeply satisfying using *The Wheel of Life*.[2]

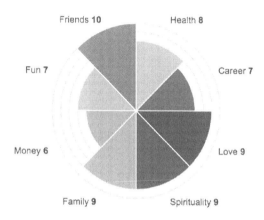

Complete the Wheel:

1. Define eight categories that are important to your life and label each segment of the blank wheel below. See my example to the right with the following categories: Friends, Health, Career, Love, Spirituality, Family, Money, and Fun.

---

[2] *Source: Adapted from Coach U resources, http://www.coachinc.com*

2. Review your eight Wheel Categories - think briefly about what a satisfying life might look like for you in each area.

3. Next, draw a line across each segment to score your satisfaction for each area.
    *   Imagine the center of the wheel is 0 and the outer edge is 10.
    *   Choose a value between 1 (very dissatisfied) and 10 (fully satisfied).
    *   Now draw a line and color in each segment of the wheel (see my example).

IMPORTANT: Use the FIRST number (score) that pops into your head, not the number you think it *should* be.

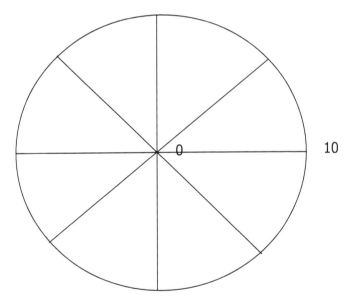

Now, looking at the wheel answer the following questions in the space below.

1. What are you surprised about?
2. How do you feel about your life as you look at your Wheel?
3. Which of these categories are you *most* satisfied with?
4. Which of these categories would you *most* like to improve?
5. How could you make space for these changes in your life?
6. What help and support might you need from others to make changes and be more satisfied with your life?
7. If there was <u>one</u> key action you could take that would begin to bring everything into balance, what would it be?

39. Challenge yourself.

Take your *Wheel of Life* results from exercise #38. Choose 3 areas that you most want to work on in the next 3 months. Identify 12 challenges (4 in each area) that will positively influence your life. Even the smallest step will set your dreams in motion. Place an "X" in each box when the challenge is completed.

Sample Focus Area: Spirituality	Focus Area #1:	Focus Area #2:	Focus Area #3:
Meditate for 15 minutes for 3 days this week.			
Write a prayer in a card and send it to a friend this week.			
Explore a new place of worship different from my own to learn new traditions.			
Study scripture and write a reflection in my journal.			

40.   Create a keepsake.

Use the final pages of this book to capture ideas, memories, and reflections from your journey in this book. Include inspirational quotes and "good things that happened" to document your progress and to keep for years to come. Below is a photo of a keepsake I created during the writing of this book to remember my journey. Take a look and create your own.

Epilogue

So now what? You've read the book. Practice the exercises. You get it. My hope is that you feel empowered to act courageously in a society that often marginalizes the gifts and dreams of many, especially women. I deeply believe that the process to access this freedom begins internally, journeys by faith, and manifests itself outwardly in powerful ways through disciplined action. This is the calling of every person's life. It's a call to fully manifest who you are.

I hope women everywhere open their hearts and minds to fresh ways to encounter and understand a liberating, nourishing and empowering God through this book. As a result, we will emerge with an affirmation of great worth despite the culture of patriarchy that still exists today.

One of my favorite characters in the bible is that of the Hebrew midwives. The midwife in biblical history fulfilled a very important function. Midwives stood in the gap between mother and child, amid life and death. That's one of the images I've held throughout my ministry and the writing of this book. Our call is a matter of life and death for women, our families and our communities. In Exodus 1:15-22, midwives sabotaged the command of the Egyptian king to kill the Hebrew boys, thus preventing genocide of a nation. Ultimately, the action of the midwives foreshadowed the Israelite's liberation from slavery in Egypt and their survival as a nation. As womanist sociologist Cheryl Townsend Gilkes said, "If it wasn't for the women there would be no exodus, no Moses, no liberation of the children of Israel of which to speak."[i]

Likewise, without women acting powerfully, the fate of ourselves, families and communities are at risk.

One of my favorite historical women leaders is Ella Baker who played a critical role in the three most prominent civil rights organizations of her day: the NAACP, the Southern Christian Leadership Conference (SCLC), and the Student Nonviolent Coordination Committee (SNCC). Through the nurturing of women in her family and the church, Baker was a courageous female leader who worked alongside the prominent male leaders of the movement and "criticized unchecked egos, objected to undemocratic structures, protested unilateral decision making, condemned elitism, and refused to nod in loyal deference to everything 'the leader' had to say. These stances often put her on the outside of the inner circle."[ii] Baker believed that, "Strong people don't need strong leaders." She argued that "oppressed people did not need a messiah to deliver them from oppression; all they needed was themselves." Her message of shared leadership was in stark contrast to the SCLC's and the Black churches patriarchal model of God.[iii]

One of my favorite contemporary women is the singer, Lauryn Hill. She was born in 1975 and represents the diversity of the postmodern actuality we live in today. Much of her music from the 1990's and early 2000's is considered "Prophetic Christianity" (a term coined by Dr. Cornell West). Her style of "conscious" rap music reflected a deeply empowering message for women while breaking down the oppressive forces of racism and sexism within the world on a spiritual level. She, like many women of the Civil Rights Movement, embodied the leadership virtues of innovation, power, and hope as she fought against the oppressive images of women in the midst of the demands of a patriarchal music industry and society. Lauryn once said in a Rolling Stone article in 2009, "The funny thing about liberation is that once you get it, anything other feels awkward." Many of her song titles over the years reflected this "Prophetic Christianity" and deep cultural consciousness such as *"Father Forgive Them"*, *"Adam Lives in Theory"*, *"To Zion"*, *"Oh Jerusalem"*, and *"The Conquering Lion"*.

Lauryn Hill's music challenged the models of what it meant to be a woman of faith in contemporary society. In fact, she redefined limitations of spirituality, combining elements of secular philosophy in a liberation theology of faith. In 2013, Lauren served a three-month prison sentence for tax evasion. Clearly, she is human and has her faults. Yet, as a mother, musician, actor, activist, and companion she represents the complexity of life as a powerful woman in the midst of challenges. Lauren, like the Hebrew midwives and Ella Baker, are warrior chicks who in their own way followed an inward and outward process of discerning, visioning, gathering, and leading powerfully. And, this journey never ends. We listen, learn, and begin a new journey in each season of our lives. We're in this together.

I invite you to continue your journey with me at www.liamcintosh.com. Join and like my Facebook page at *Coach Lia McIntosh* where you'll receive a daily #oneminuteinspiration to support your journey and find many other resources. To purchase books in bulk or request Lia as a speaker email lia@liamcintosh.com.

Lia McIntosh

About the Author

Lia McIntosh is a wife, mother, speaker, coach, writer, and community advocate.

Lia is an ordained United Methodist minister and serves as Associate Director of Congregational Excellence for the Missouri Annual Conference of the United Methodist Church. In this work, she collaborates with pastors and laity to launch new congregations and revitalize existing ones. She specializes in urban ministry and leading congregations to deeply connect with their communities. Previously, Lia served as a community organizer and pastor of four multicultural congregations.

Prior to answering her call to full-time ministry, Lia served communities across the Midwest in health care marketing and specialized in leading, training, and coaching employees. She is an International Coaching Federation (ICF) Certified Coach. She is has contributed to The Upper Room Devotional, The Abingdon Preaching Annual, and the Circuit Rider magazine.

Lia is a native of St. Louis, MO and currently lives with her husband and three children near Kansas City, MO. She is a graduate of the University of Missouri - holding a bachelor's degree and a master's degree in Business. Lia earned her Master of Divinity Degree from Saint Paul School of Theology where she now serves in the board of directors.

Above all, Lia loves God, loves God's people, and is committed to "do justice, love mercy, and walk humbly..." so that the world may be transformed!

[i] Cheryl Townsend Gilkes, *If It Wasn't for the Women…: Black Women's Experience and Womanist Culture in Church and Community* (Maryknoll, NY: Orbis, 2000).

[ii] Barbara Ransby in *Women in the civil rights movement: trailblazers and torchbearers, 1941-1965, editors* Vicki L. Crawford, Jacqueline Anne Rouse, and Barbara Woods; associate editors, Broadus Butler, Marymal Dryden, and Melissa Walker (Bloomington: Indiana University Press, 1993),, 4.

[iii] Ransby, 188.

65896020R00081

Made in the USA
Lexington, KY
27 July 2017